The New Interdependence

The New Interdependence

The European Community and the United States

Edited by
Gordon K. Douglass

Pomona College

With the collaboration of
Steven Koblik

LexingtonBooks
D.C. Heath and Company
Lexington, Massachusetts
Toronto

Library of Congress Cataloging in Publication Data

Main entry under title:
  The new interdependence.

  Proceedings of a conference organized by Pomona College and the Com-
mission of the European Communities.
  Bibliography: p.
  Includes index.
  1. European Economic Community—United States. I. Douglass, Gordon
K., 1927-   II. Koblik, Steven. III. Pomona College, Claremont, Calif. IV.
Commission of the European Communities.
HC241.25.U5N48   382'.9142'0973   79-5121
ISBN 0-669-03203-4

Copyright © 1979 by D.C. Heath and Company

Published simultaneously in Canada.

Printed in the United States of America.

International Standard Book Number: 0-669-03203-4

Library of Congress Catalog Card Number: 79-5121

To Jane

Contents

Foreword

Few words so capture the essence of our time as the word *interdependence*—the identification of a contracting, interlocked world and of the linkage between the economic, political, and security factors. A paradox arises from the parallel lack of those crucial theoretical answers to the seminal issues which interdependence raises—for example, how to achieve sustained noninflationary growth; how to strike a policy balance between the interests of the North and the South. While interdependence has become the call to arms, the world is left without a sure sense of the direction in which it is to march, or against what enemies it should do battle.

This volume, while it does not attempt to answer these basic questions, greatly helps the analytical process. It makes abundantly clear that the nation-state cannot provide the answers, indeed is one of the major obstacles to collective action. It is in this context that the existence and operation of the European Community contribute to understanding at the larger international level. The Community, with a membership of nine relatively homogeneous countries, can be seen as a laboratory model showing how certain problems that transcend national boundaries can be dealt with both in theoretical and practical terms. It can be argued that an inability to cope with these issues within the relatively congenial European Community setting raises the most serious question about the prospects for managing these same problems effectively among a vastly larger and more heterogeneous group of nations. Conversely, the Community can and should be seen as a testing ground from which other nations can benefit from the experience, the procedures, and even the failures of the institutions of the Community.

The parallels are striking between the Community and the growing international interdependence, which is the theme of the following chapters, in the sense that the Europeans have identified a substantial number of areas where common policy and collective action appear indispensable. Caught up with these problems, the Europeans have also found that the consensus on theoretical answers evades them or even when the consensus begins to emerge, national resistance to change frustrates the crucial step which is political action. One response to this dilemma has been to underscore the singular importance of the institutions of the Community, of a political system that provides the framework for the systematic analysis of problems and, over time, offers the means through which a political consensus can emerge. It was this political framework and system which enabled a European monetary system to be established after years of frustration. Similarly, as the discussion in the following pages illustrates, the new directly-elected European Parliament is in essence further evidence of the vital role of the institutions of the Community, of the belief that the new Parliament will assist in the process of both arriving at a European policy consensus and, even more importantly, providing that missing component which can mobilize Europe for political action.

There is another parallelism between the Community and the international community, especially the relationships among the advanced industrial democracies. The initial tasks of the European Community have been described as essentially negative, specifically the dismantling of tariffs and other barriers leading to a customs union and the collateral movement of stopping actions that worked against this customs union. With much of this agenda completed, the Community now faces the challenge of what can be referred to as the positive tasks; for example, developing an effective monetary system, carrying forward a regional program that will deal with the areas of major economic and social distress within the Community, devising an industrial policy that will deal in an effective and humane way with major obsolescent industries, such as shipbuilding, steel, and textiles. Similarly, the industrial democracies must move from the rather simple world of negative international activity to the much more difficult regimen of prior consultation, attention to the impact of domestic policies and programs on the interests of one's international neighbors, to the development of stronger international institutions and procedures that make the positive work of the future at least theoretically possible.

Perhaps the most striking parallel between the Community and the international scene as a whole is this paradox: At the intellectual level, the imperatives of interdependence are accepted, yet at the practical level, nations lack both the courage and the imagination to discard the "security blanket" of national prerogatives and actions. Just as the major obstacle to further progress within the European Community stems from the stubborn resistance of national governments and bureaucracies, so the process of effective international action in dealing with such critical issues as energy or the basic relationships between the rich and the poor countries gets snared by the entrenched forces of nationalism.

It is especially encouraging that Pomona College, as a distinguished educational institution of the Pacific Coast, would collaborate with the Commission of the European Community to organize the conference which is reported on in the following chapters. In addition to exposing Southern California to the extraordinary phenomenon of the European Community and to a discussion of the formidable economic issues that confront North America, Western Europe, and Japan, the conference served another major purpose. It dealt successfully with the generation gap, with the fact that the major international institutions, such as the International Monetary Fund (IMF), and the General Agreement on Trade and Tariffs (GATT), were conceived in the immediate postwar period, as was the European Community.

For the generation about to assume responsibility for these affairs, that period is no more than dim history. The conference identified that essential wedding of continuity and change. The discussions in Claremont made it abundantly clear that no matter what difficulties the world confronts, the existing policy framework, institutions, and procedures provide the indispensable point of departure for the initiatives and innovations that the present situation demands.

As a further contribution this volume insures that the conference, the work of organizing it, the efforts and contributions of those who participated in it, have been more than a passing success; the results are preserved and thus available to others. Just as Gordon Douglass so skillfully organized the Pomona conference, he and Steven Koblik provide here a commentary and synthesis that bind together the separate but related parts of the presentations made at the conference itself. If it is willing to pay attention, the international community can learn from the successes and the difficulties that confront the European Community.

One can hope as well that this experiment will encourage similar efforts elsewhere in the United States and that equally incisive examinations will be conducted of the common problems that confront our democratic societies.

J. Robert Schaetzel
U.S. Ambassador to the
European Communities, 1966-72

Preface

The seed of the idea for a conference on the new interdependence between
the European Community and the United States, as so frequently occurs,
was sown in a casual conversation—a conversation between J. Robert
Schaetzel, who kindly consented to write the foreword for this book, and
David Alexander, president of Ambassador Schaetzel's alma mater, Pomona
College. The seed germinated in broadened conversations which included
Fernand Spaak, head of the European Community delegation to the United
States, Andrew Mulligan, chief of the European Community Information
Service in Washington, D.C., and the author of this book. As discussions
widened, all of us sensed the timeliness of the topic and the importance of il-
luminating it for a broadened public.

From Pomona College's point of view, the idea of holding a conference
on the new interdependence was attractive because it would enrich the study
of international relations and related disciplines in Claremont, and because
it might forge stronger links with western audiences alert to the changing
nature of American foreign relations. College leaders saw the conference,
therefore, primarily as an academic innovation aimed at traditional college
constituencies.

It is my impression that the European Community's delegation found
interest in the conference as a means to broaden understanding among
American audiences—especially western American audiences—of the institutions and processes of the European Community, including their relationship to the vital interests of the United States. As cosponsor of the conference with Pomona College, the delegation was exceedingly helpful in at-
tracting distinguished European participants to the program. Their contributions, and those of others, are included in the conference highlights
sections of chapters 2-6.

When it came time to edit the conference proceedings, I recognized that
the telling of the story of the new interdependence was marred by two
discontinuities—or two kinds of gaps, as it were—which in fairness should
not be blamed on conference contributors. The first consists of omissions
from the conference of detailed discussions about defense and
agriculture—two important aspects of American-European interdependence. The relative absence of defense topics from discussion can
be traced institutionally to the fact that defense policies in Europe are
primarily the responsibilities of NATO and individual member governments
rather than of the Commission of the European Community, whose delegation cosponsored the conference. Thus defense issues were left out of
discussion and are not included here, except in passing references.
Agriculture, on the other hand, was lightly treated simply because we were

unable to attract to the conference the high-level European whom we had hoped would cover the topic comprehensively, and because the results of bargaining over agricultural matters during the Tokyo Round of multilateral trade negotiations were not yet clear at the time of the conference. Alas, agriculture also is shortchanged in the book.

I was better able to fill the second kind of gap in the conference transcripts—the omission of introductory materials that define interdependence—by tracing the historic evolution of interdependence, and surveying alternative strategies for dealing with it. I have tried to do this in chapter 1 and in the introductions to all subsequent chapters. Thus, as work on the manuscript progressed, it tended to take on a life of its own, separate from but complementary to the conference transcript.

This is why I feel that the book now represents a more adequate introduction to the political economy of interdependence, especially as it is played out between the United States and the countries of the European Community. It is designed both for the general reader interested in Atlantic affairs, and for students of international and comparative politics, international economics, diplomatic history, European area studies, and international relations. The new frontier is between the disciplines, or so it seems to me, and this book is meant to raise questions that defy traditional academic boundaries.

I owe my largest debt of gratitude to Professor Steven Koblik of the history department at Pomona College, who is listed as my "collaborator" on the title page of this book. This curious term was chosen to acknowledge his close association with the project from beginning to end—as cochairman with me of the conference, drafter of several portions of chapters 3 and 4, and helpful critic of successive drafts of the entire manuscript. Illness and the press of other work deprived him of the time needed to assume coauthor responsibilities.

I am grateful also to conference participants, most of whom you will find represented in the conference highlights section of the book. Their names are listed at the end of the volume in the section entitled "About the Contributors." Among them, Robert Schaetzel and Fernand Spaak deserve special acknowledgment, not only for their wise and lively contributions to conference discussions, but also for the vision they brought to the conference planning process.

Pomona College and the European Community Information Service jointly supported the conference with financial and staff contributions. Of those who helped to organize the conference, I want especially to thank Jeanette Magee and Peredita Sheirich of the Pomona College staff; Caryl McNeilly and Mark Myers who were Pomona College students at the time;

and Colin Hart, then of the European Community Information Service staff. Rose Kahalnick, Yvonne Geiger, and Mary Gammons did the typing.

It is a pleasure to have worked with all of these people on the task of better understanding the new interdependence.

1 National Interests and International Order

This book is about the process of internationalization—about the origins and meanings of what it calls the new interdependence. And it is also about the tasks governments face in devising appropriate strategies to deal with internationalization.

Modern Political Economy

Increasingly in recent years, the evolution of a strongly interdependent international economic system has been viewed as a threat to a political system that still is based primarily on the notion of sovereignty for nation-states. To be sure, rivalry beween the ends of economic and political systems has occupied the attention of national leaders many times before, leading almost continuously throughout history to attempts to reconcile economic to political goals, or vice versa. Indeed, conflicting views of mercantilists and Adam Smithian liberals about the goals of economic activity still dominate many debates among national policy-makers about the proper mix of market-directed and government-planned activities.

But the perception today that greater economic interdependence threatens governments has a quality rather different from earlier worries about conflicts between business and government. This new urgency of concern probably can be traced to two recent developments: First, the *awareness* of economic interdependence has been heightened by what seem to be larger and more frequent disturbances in the international economy, for example, global crop failures, oil cartelization, and conflicts over division of the global product and global commons; and by more violent worldwide macroeconomic instability, leaving unwanted unemployment, inflation, and sluggish growth in its wake. And secondly, domestic political *objectives* have become much more numerous, ambitious, and prone to conflict. Economic interdependence was not a serious problem before national governments began setting domestic targets for employment, price stability, growth, regional and sectoral balance, income redistribution, cleaner environment, quality of life, and a host of other social objectives.

As a result of this tension between economic interdependence and political independence, governments have been forced to devise particular strategies[1] to resist or accommodate the inexorable pressures of internationalization. One such strategy is to retreat from internationaliza-

1

tion into protectionism. This strategy has the effect of subordinating and adjusting the economic system to the demands of domestic political systems, even at the expense of sacrificing significant benefits from the rationalization of world economic activities. A protectionist strategy traditionally has been implemented by imposing general tariffs and quotas against imports. But recently the tools of protectionism have become much more selective and therefore much less efficient in their effects on resource allocation. Here, from a discouragingly long list of actively used tools, are a few examples of the ways governments protect local interests from foreign ones and even discriminate among local interests themselves: Selective fees on imports and subsidies on exports, subsidies for production and employment in certain fields and not others, public grants and preferential loans to certain producers and consumers, discriminatory product standards, the tying of foreign aid and government procurement policies to local sources of supplies, and heavier regulation of foreign-owned interests.

A second available strategy is to acknowledge the inevitability of greater international economic interdependence, but attempt to reconcile it to existing patterns of national political autonomy. One way of doing this is to develop international adjustment mechanisms, such as free-floating exchange rates and more perfect international capital markets, which operate more or less automatically when disequilibriums occur in the external economic relationships of nations. This would leave national policy-makers reasonably free to devote their energies to the pursuit of domestic objectives. Another reconciling device is to choose more carefully among available domestic policy tools for achieving particular domestic objectives so that needless cross-country distortions can be avoided. Thus, more general and less specific patterns of subsidies or taxes on investment, adjustment assistance schemes, and other devices to improve domestic resource mobility are less likely to disrupt international economic and political relations than are the tools of protectionism.

The third available strategy is to try to reconcile the existing system of national political autonomy to the increasingly international character of the economic system, by instituting a more genuine and systematic international effort toward cooperation and coordination of economic policies, especially among the leading industrial nations. This strategy may be implemented with "negative" coordination in the form of rules against certain kinds of behavior that are considered predatory, or with "positive" coordination which involves active consultation and negotiation among the nations party to the strategy. It may be as simple as the exchange of information between cooperating nations about their intended macroeconomic policies in the immediate future, or as complex as the harmonization of domestic monetary and fiscal policies among all the members of an economic and monetary union.

The idea about writing a book on the new interdependence and governmental responses to it originated at a conference held at Pomona College on March 1-3, 1978. Sponsored jointly by Pomona College and the Commission of the European Community, the conference brought together two dozen key participants from Europe and America and hundreds of interested citizens. For three days, they assessed the state of the international political-economic system, especially as it related to relations among the member states of the European Community and between members—if that is not too strong a term—of an Atlantic community, and they wondered how it was possible to resolve potential conflicts between national interests and international order at a time when governments and other international actors want more than ever to achieve their own objectives. Their conclusions, though often tentative, make interesting and provocative reading, as you will find in the conference highlights sections of chapters 2-6.

Our exploration of the new interdependence begins in the next section of this chapter with a brief history of the sources of internationalization as they have been revealed, especially in relations among European and Atlantic nations in the period since World War II. It continues in chapter 2 with a survey of the meanings of interdependence, with special attention to what have come to be called economic, strategic, political, and environmental interdependence. Chapters 3 and 4 are devoted primarily to analyses of political responses to the new interdependence. The focus of chapter 3 on the current state of the European Community permits us to identify the particular strategies adopted by political parties and governments of member nations to accommodate internationalization. Chapter 4, by contrast, looks to the future by appraising the prospects for new kinds of responses in the European Parliament as its members become directly elected for the first time.

In chapters 5 and 6, economic responses become the primary focus of discussion, as attention also broadens to include the Atlantic community and global considerations. Measures taken recently within the Atlantic community to implement the third strategy mentioned above—the coordination of economic policies by leading industrial powers—are explored in chapter 5. And attention is turned in chapter 6 to the sources of tension between developed and developing nations of the world, and to analysis of responses implicit in demands by the latter for a new international economic order.

Throughout the book, both in tone and selection of content, the authors have tried to be fair-minded about the burdens and benefits of alternative strategies to deal with the new interdependence. But readers are entitled to know that the authors brought to their task a set of normative and analytic judgments which strongly favor responses to internationalization that accord to the latter two strategies and strongly resist the first. Protectionism, particularly in the guise of highly selective "industrial policies," we believe, is even more costly in terms of efficiency and welfare than a traditional tariff system, and certainly the newer types of protectionism contain all the well-known dangers of international political strife. We doubt, moreover, that there is either evidence or acceptable theory to suggest that protectionist policies will help to alleviate the shorter-term problems now facing Atlantic nations of high unemployment rates, dangerously high inflation, and sluggish growth. In short, we believe in as liberal an order as is feasible from the effort of international coordination and cooperation and from remoulding international economic institutions to better accord to national political systems.

The Seeds of Interdependence

More than thirty years have come and gone since the end of World War II, years in which dramatic changes have occurred in the economies and polities of virtually all nations of the world. Yet relations among the nations of Western Europe and among the members of the Atlantic community continue even now to command the lion's share of attention from international scholars, diplomats, and multinational business people of western democratic societies. To be sure, tensions between East and West, North and South, have intruded insistently on these more familiar relationships, especially when fundamentally new external developments occurred, such as the evolution of new weapons systems and the cartelization of oil. And the mixture of concerns about matters of national security, economic development, political change, and environmental hazards surely shifted from time to time as a result of external pressures and events. But the equally impressive fact is that these nations of Europe and the Atlantic community have continued to sense something special in their relationships and in the potential of heightened cooperation. Our purpose here is to seek reasons why this is so.

It was not so, of course, during some periods in the past. Throughout the years between the two world wars, for example, hopes for prosperity and a durable peace in Europe were shattered, first by the vindictiveness of economic settlements made at Versailles, then by the effects of the Great Depression, and continuously in the interwar period by the unwillingness of the peoples of Europe to set aside their historic disagreements and suspicions. The United States, after helping to impose the sanctions of Versailles, returned to its policies of political isolation, and, with the onslaught of depression, reinforced them by instituting disastrously protectionist trade policies. If there was a glimmer of understanding in Europe or America that cooperation might salvage significant gains that otherwise were being lost forever, it was hard to discern in the dreary twilight of the interwar period.

The postwar experience, fortunately, is a brighter story. It is illuminated largely by two important ideas that came to shape both the patterns of European recovery following the devastation of World War II and the institutions of Atlantic cooperation throughout most of the postwar period. Both ideas were embodied in the Marshall Plan.

The first was the idea that it was in America's interest to play a key role in the revival of a working economy in the world. Instead of turning its isolationist back to Europe, which by the spring of 1947 was in a far graver state, both economically and socially, than in the thirties, America chose to support a program that was expected to cost the United States sixteen billion dollars—sixteen billion *1948* dollars! It made this major commitment, moreover, with unprecedented resolution and speed. From the time that Secretary of State George Marshall first broached the policy to his advisers and set them to work on a plan of action, only five weeks elapsed before he had announced the plan in his Harvard commencement address, and only ten months before he had encouraged the nations of Europe to design the recovery program and had gotten the U.S. Congress to enact the necessary legislative authorizations. Thus, in the words of Lord Franks, then chairman of the Committee for European Economic Cooperation which drafted the European response to America's initiative, the American policy not only was "enlightened and generous," but also "resolute and swift."

The second idea was of unity in Europe. The Marshall Plan coupled its offer of major financial assistance with conditions that compelled the nations of Europe to cooperate with one another in the drawing up of recovery plans. Accordingly, America made its offer to Europe, not just to Western Europe, letting the Soviet Union decide whether to divide Europe. The plan vested primary responsibility for the creation and execution of recovery programs in the nations of Europe, whose peoples, after all, would have to live with their consequences. It insisted that the European states develop joint programs rather than a set of unrelated national plans. And it stipulated clearly that the design of German recovery had to be an integral part of any jointly designed program, lest the economic recovery of Europe as a whole would falter in the absence of improvements in German productivity.

The idea of working toward a more fully integrated Europe was not solely an American dream, it should be stressed. The Committee for European Economic Cooperation freely acknowledged the interdependence of the European economies throughout its report, a linkage that it imagined might very well be increased by technological developments which occurred during the war and which were likely to yield greater economies of scale in postwar civilian applications. In an especially prescient chapter, the report even encouraged study of the potential for a Europe-wide customs union to combat the then-current fragmentation of European economic activities.

And by early in 1948, when the convention establishing the Organization for European Economic Cooperation (OEEC), later to be known as the Organization for Economic Cooperation and Development (OECD) was being drafted, Europe's leaders already were debating the relative advantages of OEEC under the control of the participating governments—the British conception—and a more powerful and centralized OEEC with authority to coordinate the activities of member countries and to take major initiatives in policy—the French conception. By then, clearly, the issue had become not whether, but how to coordinate European economic activities.

Nor should the idea of unity for Europe be interpreted solely, or even primarily, as a set of economic objectives. There is no doubt, of course, that economic recovery from the devastation of World War II and fuller economic integration of the nations of Western Europe were objectives that political leaders on both sides of the Atlantic broadly shared. Unity in Europe was important for economic reasons. But these leaders also saw unity as a means of achieving other important objectives which, though closely linked to the revitalization of the European economy, are better described as social and political motives for trans-Atlantic cooperation.

Perhaps the foremost of these was the urge to diminish the causes of war in Western Europe. Of all the motives for European unity, this one seems least remembered today, after thirty years of peace in Western Europe. Yet at war's end, memories of the rivalry between states (such as Germany and France) that had so often plunged the continent into conflict were hideously fresh, motivating the peoples of Europe to search for ways to reconcile their differences permanently. Peace through interdependence became their dominant vision.

Another urgent objective of a political sort was the need to strengthen security in the Atlantic community against attack by the military forces of the Soviet Union. This could be accomplished, it was thought, by building a strong and united economy in Western Europe and by establishing institutions for unified Western military preparedness that could force the Soviets to incur significant costs if they launched attacks against Western Europe. Accession by the United States to the North Atlantic Treaty confirmed the leading role it was destined to play in Atlantic military affairs.

And still a third important noneconomic reason for Atlantic cooperation was to preserve and strengthen democratic political processes in Western Europe. Except in Great Britain and Scandinavia, one European democratic institution after another had given way to political absolutism during the thirties, leaving the countries of Europe perilously close to fundamentally undemocratic forms of government. After the war, a new threat to democratic institutions was feared, this time from the Left rather than the Right, especially from the Communist parties of Italy and France. Once again, rapid economic recovery and movements toward political unity were thought to provide Western Europeans with the likeliest opportunities to reestablish democratic polities.

These two ideas—Atlantic cooperation and unity in Europe—not only inspired the Marshall Plan, but were also instrumental for the better part of two decades in guiding many key relationships among the Western industrial democracies. One saw their influence, for example, in the design of such institutional innovations as the arrangements of the late forties and early fifties for intra-European trade liberalization and intra-European monetary settlement, in the movement of the fifties toward economic integration—especially in the formation of the European Coal and Steel Community (ECSC) and a few years later, the European Economic Community (EEC) and the European Atomic Energy Community (Euratom)—and in the evolutionary changes of the OECD, following its accession to the important work of the OEEC in 1960. And one could sense from the processes of diplomacy during the fifties and early sixties that the primary international actors, by and large, still behaved as if there were substantive consensus on the desirability of Atlantic cooperation and European unity.

The New Interdependence

But it would be silly to suppose that the quality of the Atlantic commitment to cooperation and unit remained constant while objective conditions in the economies and polities of Atlantic nations and the rest of the world changed dramatically in the sixties and seventies. At the beginning of the postwar period, the United States was clearly the dominant central power in the Atlantic relationship—the only victor of the war to have emerged with greater power and wealth. It faced the Soviet enigma across a prostrate Europe, and the rest of the world hardly counted at all. Then, rallying with the Marshall Plan medicine, the European economies began to grow, rapidly at first by repairing damaged and neglected capital equipment and reforming outdated systems of control, still more rapidly later through a deepened commitment to saving and capital formation, and to the rationalization of European labor supplies. Their growth, aided by the closer economic ties of membership in the European communities, outpaced that of the United States and brought their collective economic strength, if not their uses of power, to a parity with that of America by the end of the sixties. This dramatic closure of economic disparities within the Atlantic community, and with it the gradual eclipse of America's earlier postwar role as leader of the community, is by itself grounds for expecting refinements in European and American attitudes toward cooperation and unity.

But economic convergence was not all that happened to alter these attitudes. The very processes of growth and change in Europe that engineered convergence were also responsible for a considerable deepening of the links among national and regional economies, both within Europe, where the institutions of economic integration systematically lowered the barriers to economic intercourse among nations, and throughout the world, where revolutionary advances in the technology of communication, production, and distribution rapidly transformed the conditions for profitable economic exchange. It is the latter sources of transnational linkages, indeed, that proably best explain the use of the term *new* in the title of this book.

One hardly can overemphasize the transforming quality of these dramatic technological advances. In particular, technological innovations in communications made transmission of printed, spoken, and visual images virtually instantaneous and lowered their cost to a fraction of previous levels. These revolutionary developments integrated markets for financial assets as well as for tradeable goods and services, permitting a much higher degree of substitution among them than ever before. They also were instrumental in the internationalization of entrepreneurship and the diffusion across international borders of new technological achievements in production and distribution—two essential conditions for the efficient operation of global organizations. The advent of multinational corporate activities on a vastly wider basis than before thus became both the promise and the curse of the new interdependence.

In addition to these remarkable economic trends, the peoples of the Atlantic community experienced dramatic changes in their perception of social needs during the period of rapid European recovery and growth. Increasing affluence has a way of raising aspirations and making prominent in the political arena a series of issues—the environment, air and noise pollution, the redistribution of income, the quality of life in general—that require governments instead of markets to reconcile competing interests and adjudicate conflicting claims. National governments no longer enjoyed the luxury of dealing primarily with issues such as law and order, it seemed, about which consensus was much easier to achieve; "tradeoffs" between interest groups became the rule rather than the exception. Some of the new items on lists of perceived needs, moreover, required for their solutions the mutual agreement of several governments, which is to say that some of the external effects of production and consumption, such as air and ocean pollution, overfishing, and the demonstration of consumption habits, became internationalized, external not only to business firms or households, but also to nations. Thus, governments of leading industrial countries, in the word of one sociologist, were increasingly "overloaded" with the conflicting demands of modern affluent society during the last decade or two.

To be sure, governments tried hard not to be placed in the position of choosing between the objectives of interest groups that represented significant parts of their constituency. One way to avoid some tradeoffs, they reasoned, was to match the burgeoning list of domestic objectives with an augmented inventory of policy tools for achieving them; and what could be more natural as a source of supply of new policy tools than the devices of foreign policy. Just as mathematicians will seek more equations when the number of unknowns increases, practical politicians instinctively will develop new "instrumental" variables when the number of "target" variables multiplies. It is not very surprising, therefore, that as the sixties and seventies ushered in a period of fractious national politics, many governments, few of which had ever been very clear about the distinction between domestic and foreign policies, allowed the pursuit of domestic objectives to intrude more and more into the making of foreign policies.

Even so, the tendency to see government policy decisions as tradeoffs against other potential objectives grew rapidly in advanced industrial countries. Bureaucrats caught in the middle of conflicting claims, and the interest groups most likely to reap direct benefits or incur direct costs from the implementation of particular policies, saw more clearly than most citizens, perhaps, that choices among competing objectives had to be made and that their impact on the distribution of wealth and power at home and abroad would surely be significant. But the general citizenry soon learned from the course of events that they, too, had a stake in the outcome of government deliberations that decided what objectives to pursue. Single-issue interest groups arose in all industrial countries to plead their cases before the public and its representatives in government.

The event that probably best explains more than any other the giving up by more and more citizens of a benign view of government was the slackening of growth rates in the early seventies, not only in Europe but in most of the industrial world. The immediate cause of sluggish growth rates seemed to be fears engendered by the prospect of higher rates of inflation—fears, on the one hand, that there was little opportunity in an interdependent world (short of cutting nations off from the benefits of international intercourse) to resist the intrusion into domestic markets of inflation originating abroad, and fears, on the other hand, that the increasingly fragmented and cynical domestic polity of most nations had neither the will nor the ability to act decisively against inflation at home. And even if the will to control inflation could be found, some felt, its implementation was likely in the short run to lead to a recession. By creating uncertainty in the minds of both savers and investors, these fears weakened, at least temporarily, the conditions for constant growth. Slackened growth and the prospect of recession, in turn, no doubt forced further refinements in European and American attitudes toward cooperation and unity, by diminishing the capacity of the

Atlantic economies to generate mutually advantageous gains from working together.

Nor has the rest of the world stood still while the nations of the Atlantic community reassessed the closeness of their interests. Japan's phenomenal growth in the postwar period, for instance, created yet another powerful economic actor in world markets and added still more complexity to the foreign relations of Atlantic nations. Another example of the changing environment of Atlantic relations was the balance of mutual threat achieved and maintained by the American and Soviet superpowers. This standoff in military security affairs reduced the relative importance of traditional security issues on the agenda of world politics and reinforced the tendencies to pay more attention to the issues that are central to domestic politics—the issues of economic growth and social welfare. And yet another illustration of changes in the world environment was the emergence of several new centers of power in the developing world—some the result of harvesting the fruits of cartel actions and some the effect of successful development programs. Their roles in world politics, previously largely ignored by the industrial powers, have recently taken on new urgency as they have begun to champion the causes of poorer states in the articulation of demands for a new international economic order.

In all of these ways—and more—the contexts of European unity and Atlantic cooperation have changed in recent years, creating for member states both new *restrictions* on their capacities to achieve domestic objectives and interests by acting unilaterally, and new *opportunities* (even while feigning cooperation with other nations) to sponsor their own private or governmental interests. Thus, all nations have learned from sometimes bitter experience that changes in the money supply, credit conditions, or taxation policies of one country in order to stabilize its economy can easily generate unexpected international movements of capital, exports and imports, and prices that will frustrate the intended purposes of policy changes in the first place. The greater the linkages between national partners, the more likely that decisions made in one country, whether by governments or private economic interests, will influence the economies of the others. Interdependence in this sense restricts the freedom of states to attain desirable domestic objectives independently, and encourages the search for more unified and cooperative strategies.

Somewhat paradoxically, the new interdependence also provides some nations with heightened opportunities to promote distinctively national interests. These opportunities may take any of several forms: The expansion of markets for certain products, such as German automobiles, French aircraft, Japanese electronic goods, and American grain, which for one reason or another suit them particularly well for export; the promotion of profit opportunities for multinational enterprises, whose possession of rare skills or resources encourages them to expand globally; and the exploitation by governments of privileged positions in order to achieve otherwise unattainable concessions from partner countries, such as the bargaining done by France and Britain over the European Community's Common Agricultural Policy (CAP) to obtain aid for injured consumers and backward regions, and the use of the oil weapon by Arab nations to alter the foreign policies of oil-importing industrial nations.

Since the new interdependence both restricts and enhances the opportunities of nations to pursue their national interest, the art of managing interdependence has become one of manipulating the processes of linkage in ways that both minimize the restrictions felt by particular nations on their freedom to seek national objectives, and maximize the availability of opportunities provided by the new interdependence to further the national interest. Or, as we stated the matter strategically at an earlier point in the chapter, the art of managing interdependence has become, to a very considerable extent, one of reconciling international integration to the existing system of national politics that accords highest merit to the achievement of national purposes.

The problems with this strategy are twofold. In the first place, nations are inherently unequal in their abilities to influence the design of institutions that are meant to permit this kind of compromise between economic and political ends, and they are also vastly different in their abilities to make use of existing institutions to further their own ends. As in so many other questions involving international relations, skill and power make a difference. Thus the process that has led to successive revisions in the institutions of international economic integration—exchange rate regimes, systems of international settlement, international trading and investment systems, conventions governing the movement of peoples and ideas internationally, and others—has tended to be dominated by the strongest and cleverest nations, much as the more traditional model of "realist" world politics assigned the lion's share of advantage to the mighty. It is no great leap of imagination to suppose, therefore, that the strongest nations may actively promote the adoption of strategies that encourage international cooperation and coordination because they have confidence that they can manage the system to their *relative* advantage. For this reason, it is occasionally hard to tell on first reading of the conference highlights which alternative strategy is uppermost in each speaker's mind.

A strategy that attempts to reconcile international economic integration to demands for autonomy of existing political systems has the second disadvantage of thinking about the costs and benefits of interdependence in static terms. The benefits or new opportunities of interdependence are not only gains achieved at the expense of weaker and less skillful nations. Just as possibly, they may be gains achieved cooperatively through better organization of the international economy and with improved coordination in dealing with shared political problems—gains, as it were, that are created rather than stolen frm another country. The economic gains from specialization in production and trade and from the easy flow of messages and ideas internationally probably constitute the primary means since World War II of assuring mutual gains for the players on the world politics chessboard. But the newly identified need to coordinate the uses of macroeconomic stabilization tools may well be yet another major source of advantage for all nations. The loss of potential output from poorly managed and coordinated monetary and fiscal policies in recent years is staggering.

Yet the vision of mutual gain from international cooperation seems to require more than a simple commitment to the benefits of economic integration. The ideas of Atlantic cooperation and European unity which so anchored the Marshall Plan and so dominated Atlantic diplomatic relations in the fifties and sixties had sprung not only from economic understanding but very especially, as noted above, from a common concern for military security and a common desire to preserve democratic political institutions. Together, these motives were enough to seal the bargains that produced European recovery, transformed Atlantic institutions, and animated the close feelings of Americans and Europeans for each other through much of the postwar period.

In a world of changing environments and competing calculations, it seems proper, therefore, to ask whether there is enough commonness of will remaining in the Atlantic community to continue the quest for Atlantic cooperation and European unity. The immediate threat of military conquest by the Soviet Union seems no longer to dominate the agenda of Western statesmen. The fascist and communist threats to the political institutions of Europe seem also to have subsided. And even the lengendary gains of market growth and integration have come into question, the victims of changing social values, which seem now to accord greater concern to the goals of economic and social stability and distributional fairness, and of doubts arising mostly in developing countries about the "neutrality" of an economic system that apparently benefits rich more than poor peoples and nations.

There is no easy answer to the question. The participants at Pomona College's conference on the new interdependence certainly made clear in their remarks that the need for cooperation and coordination is greater today than ever. A common will *must* be found, they said, lest international relations in the Atlantic community deteriorate into "disorganized anarchy." But from what inner fires will it come? one persists. Probably from the continuing assimilation of knowledge about what has been accomplished cooperatively over these last decades, and from the experience of dealing with future crises when the painful alternatives to cooperation become better understood. This is not a time for grand designs, they agreed, but only for prayer that the legacy of the Marshall Plan will see us through these fractious days.

Note

1. For an especially helpful survey of available strategies, see Assar Lindbeck, "Economic Dependence and Interdependence in the Industrialized World," pp. 83-86.

2

Meanings of
Interdependence

Most national policy-makers have always been aware of the influence of foreign developments on their own problems, and policy-makers especially of larger countries have recently been made increasingly aware of the impact of their own decisions on others. The latter fact, even for a country as traditionally self-sufficient as the United States, requires residents as well as policy-makers in the Western industrial countries to better understand the nature and meanings of the new interdependence. Whether of economic, political, cultural, or security origins, interdependence demands of us all that we see the world as smaller, yet infinitely more complex, than we had previously imagined it could be.

Economic Interdependence

The most specific element of the new interdependence is the tangled web of economic relationships in which virtually all countries are increasingly enmeshed. In the social scientists' jargon, the "low politics" of goods and money has replaced the "high politics" of military security affairs as the premier concern of national governments in this period of lower international "threat perception." The speakers at the conference, represented in this chapter by Sir Christopher Soames, Dr. Robert Solomon, and Senator Alan Cranston, made this point abundantly clear, even while noting the numerous points at which this web of economic interdependence links up with the network of political, cultural, and security ties among nations that until recently have preoccupied the time of senior governmental officials, especially in the leading western nations of Europe, North America, and Japan.

    Economic interdependence most commonly has been thought to have heightened on the evidence of rapidly growing numbers of international economic transactions during the last two or three decades. Movements of goods and services, people, money capital, and enterprises across international borders have been multiplied time and time again since the end of hostilities in World War II. The growth in international trade and payments has greatly outpaced the measures of international output, and the advent of world-spanning operations by multinational enterprises has transformed the nature of business decisions. There is no doubt that the volume of international economic transactions has risen tremendously in both absolute and relative terms.

In the conference highlights of this chapter, Robert Solomon adds historical perspective to this evidence by noting that international economic transactions have been growing relative to output ever since the beginning of the Industrial Revolution nearly two hundred years ago—with the notable exception of a period spanning two world wars and a great depression in the earlier part of this century. Interdependence measured in this way is not a new phenomenon, he argues, despite assertions to the contrary shortsightedly based on the evidence of interwar experience alone. To be sure, the long-term expansion of international economic transactions has recently been accompanied by qualitative changes that can, on the evidence, be considered relatively new. They include the intensification of trade among industrial countries, the rapid growth of manufacturing in an increasing number of developing countries, and an increase in the mobility of money capital among industrial countries. But the quantitative rise in international transactions of all kinds, when compared to the volume of production, is very long-lived indeed.

The volume of international transactions, however, is not the only, nor even the most important, measure of international economic interdependence. A second widely used index of economic interdependence, to which all conference participants referred, is the degree to which economic events in one country are sensitive to what is happening in other nations. All elements of a national economy are exposed in one way or another to events that originate outside the nation's borders. Individual consumers, workers, investors, businesses, or financial institutions can be aided or damaged by changes in the flow of trade, travel, worker migration, foreign investment, and financial capital. Whole economies can be made better or worse by the expansion or contraction of economic activity in another nation. Changes in government policy abroad and, in reaction to them, policy changes at home, can significantly influence both micro- and macroeconomic outcomes at home.

Although it seems plausible to suppose that changes in the volume of international transactions, and in their relationship to aggregate production, might influence the degree of sensitivity felt by particular nations to events originating abroad, there seems no reason to believe that these two measures of economic interdependence are perfect substitutes. If, for example, the share of exports and imports in gross national product (GNP) doubles, feelings of exposure to external events surely need not double also, unless by coincidence. Far too many characteristics of the nation and its environment influence its sense of exposure to allow us to expect such lockstep. Indeed, even as international transactions have multiplied, studies that have attempted directly to measure economic sensitivities have found very little change in sensitivity over time.

Perhaps the best historical explanation for this lack of symmetry in the leading measures of economic interdependence is that the volume of international transactions of a country really focuses on the gains or benefits of international intercourse, whereas measures of the degree of sensitivity to external disturbances tend to focus on the tensions and costs associated with exposure to international events. Historically, the benefits of trading, investing, and migrating have been thought to be very large indeed. Undergirded by liberal international trade theory, the notion that international specialization yields vast benefits in the form of heightened productivity, enhanced output, greater variety, and more innovation for *all* participating nations has provided the main intellectual foundations of the dominant liberal trading policies of Europe and America for the last half-century. Sir Christopher's testament to the liberal tradition is included in the text of his remarks. The costs of adjusting to new patterns of comparative advantage were not ignored in liberal theory; they simply were assumed to be vastly outweighed by the gains from specialized international intercourse.

Recently, however, governments seem to have perceived that the costs of adjustment are mounting. Faced with new demands by their constituents for a more equitable income distribution and for a vast array of new social services, they have sought increasingly effective controls of their own destinies. While some sectors and individuals of national economies still benefit enormously from economic intercourse with the outside world, others perceive that they do not. Dramatic shifts in the sentiment of organized American labor toward protectionism is perhaps the clearest case in point. Thus even some, who in general still affirm comparative advantage analysis, now question whether the structural and frictional unemployment and other adjustment costs accompanying increased rates of change in the distribution of productive activities among countries and industries can much longer be tolerated politically. The evidence of research findings about measured economic sensitivities to the contrary, many people now *perceive* a new level of interdependence, and are seeking ways, in Richard Cooper's words, "to keep the manifold benefits of extensive economic intercourse free of crippling restrictions while at the same time preserving a maximum degree of freedom for each nation to pursue its legitimate economic objectives."[1]

Yet another measure of economic interdependence—this one promoted more by political scientists than by economists—is the degree to which countries rely upon each other for goods and services that cannot be easily produced at home. This seems to be what Robert Solomon means by "mutual vulnerability" and what others refer to as "mutual dependence." In economic terms, the concept thus limits the sense of economic interdependence to those international transactions which would, if stopped, impose heavy "opportunity costs" on nations deprived of vital supplies.

Perhaps the best illustrations of the relevance of this concept are the Arab oil embargo and oil price increases of 1973-74. They surely did more to create the impression of vulnerability to external events than any other international development of the last dozen years. As a result, the oil-importing countries are incurring considerable extra costs to develop alternative energy sources, both to cut down on their dependence on the reliability of supplies from the Middle East and to acknowledge the possibility of reserve depletion in the foreseeable future. The oil-importing countries fell hostage not only to the Organization of Petroleum Exporting Countries (OPEC) suppliers, but also to each other, since actions by any one country that alter demand or supply conditions in the international marketplace influence the length of time all other nations will have to complete long-run adjustments. Even the OPEC suppliers sense heightened interdependence, both in their capacities as members of a cartel that can remain effective only through an agreement among its members to coordinate pricing and supply decisions, and in their positions as newly developing nations dependent on their chief customers for industrial and agricultural imports, the supply of new technologies, and the services of financial intermediaries to invest and manage their vast balance of payment surpluses.

National reactions to the OPEC crises remind us that the perception of economic interdependence depends not only upon the sensitivity of nations to external events, but also upon the frequency and magnitude of such events. One wonders whether the frequency of recent international convulsions—of oil embargoes and price increases, poor harvests, worldwide depression, hyperinflation, heightened expectations, and so on—may not have influenced the sense of interdependence even more than their individual effects on domestic economic and political affairs. It is entirely possible that the perception of interdependence is as much the simple expression of helplessness, of the sense that domestic attitudes and institutions no longer have enough time to adjust gracefully before the onslaught of yet another unmanageable disturbance originating elsewhere in the world, as it is the perception of costs imposed from abroad which can be eliminated or reduced eventually by clever policy changes at home.

Political Interdependence

This takes us directly to the concept of political interdependence. In recent years, both the nature of large international disturbances and the channels through which their shocks have been transmitted to individual countries have created forms of interdependence that no longer can be managed by taking unilateral action at home. As Senator Cranston points out later in this chapter, a variety of international organizations have been formed to share the burdens of adjustment and to develop a set of political instruments that can better meet the needs of nations for a stable international environment. Some of these organizations seem best to fit the strategic model that reconciles the forces of economic integration to domestic political realities, such as agreement by the International Monetary Fund (IMF) to flexible exchange rates, whereas others accord primarily to a strategy of cooperation that surrenders some domestic political autonomy to the tasks of achieving common objectives.

The experiences of the European Community in forming cooperative international political organizations, which we will turn to in greater detail in chapter 3, are perhaps the best contemporary illustrations of the trials of political interdependence. The struggle for legitimacy of European Community institutions has been intense and prone to delays. Though these institutions were created to solve specific problems thought to be unmanageable by national decision alone, they have been denied full support for these tasks by the very nation-states that created them. The reason is that politics in Europe are intensely national, indeed even regional and local. Political leaders who recognize the need for European solutions to certain problems, therefore, frequently have difficulty sustaining domestic support for their efforts. As a result, recent attempts to renew progress toward common monetary policies and toward a politically legitimate European parliament are unlikely to be fully or immediately successful.

Having established many international political and economic institutions in the postwar period, the nations of the Atlantic community ought by now to be able to recognize that their common institutions create opportunities as well as restrictions on their freedom of action. At the governmental level, affiliation with international institutions sometimes has permitted national governments to achieve domestic political objectives that were otherwise elusive. After France joined the European Community, for example, it harnessed the competitive forces of freer trade and migration to the task of transforming antiquated French business practices, and with them, undesirable domestic political conditions. When the IMF in another set of examples, "imposed" severe budgetary and social policy restrictions on the British and Italian governments in 1977, its actions were used by these governments to free themselves from commitments to socialist ideologues in one case, and numerous domestic pressure groups in the other. In yet another illustration from an earlier period, it has been argued that the Eisenhower administration supported the formation of the European Community, at least in part, as a means of creating economic conditions in Europe that would shift the distribution of income away from workers and toward capitalists, and thus would swing the balance of European political power toward governments more friendly to (Eisenhower's and Dulles's vision for) the United States.

The forms of interdependence also have been used by nongovernmental interests to achieve their own objectives. Access to the channels of interdependence has permitted the news media, unions, trade associations, professional groups, intellectuals, and a host of other private actors—as well, of course, as legions of multinational enterprises—to gain easier contact with the political and economic elites in other countries, and to extend their ability to manipulate behavior in other countries. Political interdependence thus becomes a private as well as a governmental phenomenon, reinforcing the possibility that nations with the greatest ability to deal with political and social forces abroad may gain relative advantages in a cooperating world.

Questions of Security

In security as in economic affairs, the interdependence of nations has been growing, with minor exceptions, for a very long time. The alliance system prior to 1914, and the joint military efforts of two world wars were expressions of this interdependence. So, too, were the North Atlantic Treaty Organization (NATO) and Warsaw Pact alliances following World War II—alliances made especially urgent by the advent of advanced nuclear weaponry. Even neutral states such as Sweden, Switzerland, and Austria are sensitive to the fact that their security is dependent primarily on the nature of military relations between the East and West.

Nonetheless, some nations apparently feel more bound than secure in these interdependencies. France in NATO and Rumania in the Eastern bloc both have questioned the effectiveness and fairness of existing security alliances, and both have been particularly critical of the dominant roles played, respectively, by the United States and the Soviet Union in their defense blocs.

Sophisticated weapons are rarely the product of a single nation. Typically, parts and components from several countries will be combined in the assembly of particular weapons systems. The reasons are both economic and political: Some weapons systems are so costly to develop and are produced with such significant economies of scale and of learning, that each key component of the system must be produced in a single location. Yet each completed system must be sold widely in order to recover production costs. Accordingly, the weapons industry, in conjunction with client nations, has come to depend on a structure of bargaining that allocates subcontracts for parts and components among the key purchasers of completed systems. The recent sale of American fighter planes to its NATO allies is an appropriate example. Belgium and the Netherlands needed advanced interceptors. Their choice among three alternative models was based both on performance characteristics and on evaluation of the relative economic benefits associated with sharing in each model's production. In the event, the victorious American company won prime contracts with the help of promises to arrange procurement of important components in the purchasing states. Having won the NATO contracts, moreover, it obtained a special advantage in the development of the next generation of planes. Thus, the interdependence of nations for mutual security may, in fact, be even larger than politicians sometimes confess.

The comments of Senator Cranston and Sir Christopher clearly identify the need to see security and economic interdependence as related parts of a growing international linkage of developed industrial countries. Both speakers seem to be saying that European-American economic ties and security relations have reinforced one another as they have grown since World War II. Dr. Hara, whose remarks appear in chapter 5, implies a similar relationship between Japanese-American economic and security conditions. These signs of overlapping interdependence are reinforced, of course, by the ideological similarities of the primary industrial democracies, a point that Sir Christopher stresses in particular.

The developing states, by contrast, seem to have been moving toward more self-reliant national security measures, given the technical and organizational demands of warfare most likely to develop in their part of the world. Even so, these newly developing nations have had to take account of the attitudes of patron nations toward national security entanglements, lest local conflicts influence adversely the economic interdependence they feel so acutely with developed nations.

Environmental Interdependence

Finally, there seems to be a growing awareness of environmental interdependence. Everyone, regardless of nationality, depends on harvests from the global commons, including the air we breathe, sunlight, outer space, the earth's heat, the seabed, the high seas and international straits, and fuel and nonfuel minerals. Some of these resources are not governed yet by particular nations, and none of them, as illustrations of what economists call "market failure," will prove to be self-adjusting if its exploitation is left entirely to world market processes. In some cases, pollution drifts from one nation's jurisdiction to another. In others, ships pollute the ocean with oil and deplete ocean fisheries by overfishing. Externalities of these sorts seem pervasive in the modern world, spilling over from country to country and requiring the special attention of multinational groups lest innocent people suffer or free riders benefit without paying.

Conference Highlights

The New Interdependence of Europe
Sir Christopher Soames

The principle of interdependence has been with us since early times. The interdependence of families, of tribes, of regions within a nation, are no doubt very ancient indeed. But it is only since the war, really, that interdependence has grown to be an international phenomenon of major importance to us all.

I suppose the Marshall Plan was an early example of the recognition of international interdependence. Sir Winston Churchill referred to it as the most unsordid action that any country has ever taken. And it was basically an altruistic action. But it was also a matter of interest that the United States undertake it. Without in any way trying to detract from the generosity both of thought and of action that underlay the Marshall Plan, I think the United States clearly wanted to rebuild for their own purposes the economies of the European countries and the prosperity of their peoples after the ravages of war.

The European Community is probably the prime contemporary example of interdependence of a commercial, economic, and political character. It is commercial and economic because we all came to realize, some earlier than others, that the nation-state of fifty million or fewer peoples which made up the countries of Western Europe could no longer use commercial or economic clout sufficiently to influence the world in a manner they thought benign. By getting together in a community and making certain rules, the founding fathers thought they could aspire to having the influence to which the states of Europe were accustomed in the world.

It began, in fact, in the European Coal and Steel Community, but was planned to grow as an economic community and to become eventually a political community. All of us in Western Europe appreciated the fact that it was in our homelands that the two world wars had started, and that we must knit together our economies so that no country could dream of making war ever again.

Now what effect has the European Community had upon countries of the Community and upon the lives of its peoples? From a commercial and economic point of view, I think there is no doubt of the prosperity derived from the movement of Europe toward a single, unified, outward-looking market. Without that movement toward economic integration, the great advance in productivity of European industry and agriculture could never have been achieved. Without it we could not have been the source of opportunities through specialization to rationalize production and distribution, reap the economies of scale, and heighten the confidence necessary for large-scale investment. There would not have been the same spur toward technological innovation or the same incentives for greater efficiency. In short, without the wider European markets of now 250 million people, there would have been fewer jobs and fewer opportunities during the happy years of growth from 1960 to 1973.

And what about the bad times? Has Europe been a benign influence during bad times too, such as the period of recession since 1973? Certainly during these difficult years since the middle of 1973, the Community has been a force against protectionism both inside its borders and throughout the rest of the world. Within the Community, no member country has dared to put up trade barriers without at least the permission of its partners. As a community that has to live by trading with the outside world, it also has been in our interest to do our very best, in spite of the political difficulties that weighed upon us, to be an example against protectionism.

This leads me to consider the question of the general effects of the Community upon the outside world. How much power does it have? Military power is not the only form of power that matters in the present-day world, and I think it valuable to recognize how very considerable is the economic power of the Community of the Nine. We have a GNP that is not far short of the United States. The member states of the Community do no less than 40 percent of all the trade of the free world. We have 30 percent of the world's currency reserves. We provide 40 percent of the official development assistance and a large proportion of private investment and new technology for the Third World. And for many countries, we are the most important export market, particularly for food and raw materials.

These statistics of economic strength are all the more remarkable because of the suddenness with which the Community has gained its power. One would think that for a country to arrive at such a point, it would need generations or centuries of working at it and of learning to live with others. It didn't happen that way for the Community. We emerged as an economic force, with all the potential political power that accompanies it, from one day to the next in historical terms; we were parachuted into the world. The Community of Six has been going now for twenty years, the Community of the Nine, for only five. Had we come about more gradually, we would have learned to live with other countries more confidently.

It is small wonder, therefore, that countries, both great and small, asked themselves how this new economic and commercial monster was going to affect their national fortunes. I always thought that the influence the Community was going to bear toward the outside world would be in direct proportion to the extent to which it learned to reach its conclusions of a political character jointly and express them with one voice. That was the yardstick in international terms.

We have gone part way toward this goal. We have a common commercial policy and a common agricultural policy, for example. But we have a long way to go yet, considering the fact that all nine countries have their own histories, their own pride, and God knows, their own prejudices. They still see many things through nationalists' eyes. As the French say, we've eaten the white bread. But when it comes to energy policies (does this ring a bell with you?), we have found it difficult to persuade the Nine to develop a common policy. There are, I'm afraid, lots of other examples like this. Economic and monetary union still eludes us, and without that it is indeed hard to see Europe growing as a real factor in world affairs.

How have we behaved toward the outside world? Were they right to be fearful of us? Has our sense of interdependence grown as the limits of our power over others became apparent? Let's look for answers to these questions in the policies of the Community toward just two parts of the world at large—the countries that are still struggling to develop, and the United States. They're surely enough to go on with.

We have not been evenhanded with the Third World. We are the prisoners of our own past. During the creation of the Community of Six, France insisted that for historical reasons special treatment had to be given to those countries of French-speaking Africa that depended on trade with France for their very livelihood. The result was the Yaoundé Convention. And when it came time to enlarge the Community, Britain felt that it had similar responsibilities to countries in anglophile Africa, and so the Yaoundé Convention became the Lomé Convention. We handle the rest of the developing world as you do through the Generalized Scheme of Preferences (GSP). But even here, not all countries have equal access to Community markets. We have, in fact, so tailored our GSP as to assure that the trade for certain countries with the Community, particularly the Indian subcontinent and Southeast Asia, would not be damaged by virtue of Community enlargement.

We have the feeling, I must say, of being more interdependent with the Third World than the United States seems to be. Why should this be so? First of all, we depend in the Community to a far larger extent than does the United States on the provision of raw materials from the Third World. As we have to export a very high proportion of our GNP in order to survive in this world, we also look to the Third World to provide us, as time goes by, with a growing market for our goods.

This reason for feeling more interdependent with the Third World has been reinforced by recent experience in the recession we seem unable to stop. The period of growth in the sixties was rather incestuous inasmuch as it boosted trade among the developed nations and widened the gap between the developed and developing worlds. I think a lesson has been learned in this recession, that for long-term, sustained growth in all our countries, we no longer can depend so heavily on trading just among ourselves. We need to look for other growing markets in the developing world.

Now a word about our relationship with the United States. In spite of the fact that successive U.S. governments have supported the European idea and the concept and enlargement of the Community, I still detected a certain anxiety over here. Successive U.S. administrations seem to have been saying: "We understand about U.S.-French relations, U.S.-German relations, and U.S.-British relations, but how is the Community going to act?" I think it was anxiety that led, if you remember, to 1973 being declared by the U.S. administration as the Year of Europe. I must say, I rang up a friend of mine in the U.S. administration and said, "I promise you one thing, we won't make 1974 the Year of America." I think we have to go on living together, and we're going to have to go on understanding each other. Interdependence can't be switched on and off like a light bulb.

How have the United States and the Community worked out their relations in the event? Of course, there have been differences of a commercial character, mostly about access to markets. The U.S. administration doesn't like our agricultural policy, and the Community is worried about the U.S. countervailing duties that can be imposed without proof of injury to U.S. industries. And we feel sometimes that the balance between national and sectional interests, on one hand, and international responsibilities, on the other, is not always struck properly in America. Even so, we have held well together so far.

How does one see the relationship developing in the future between the United States and the Community? First of all, we both must stand fast against protectionism, and the longer the recession lasts, the harder this is going to be. Second, we must understand each other, and particularly each other's limitations. There are a lot of built-in misunderstandings, and one has to be able to put oneself in the skin of the other country. This is why we need so desperately people with international experience.

Third, let's not get too heated up in advance about issues that are unlikely to arise, such as the power of Eurocommunism in Europe. If any member country of the Community ever got itself a government that ceased to follow precepts of a pluralist democracy and the freedoms that they involve, then that country could no longer remain a member of the Community. And none of our member states can afford to leave the Community. We've got enough difficulties already without thinking up new ones that don't exist yet.

Fourth, we must leave the Soviet Union with absolutely no doubt whatsoever that an attack upon Western Europe would mean the whole of NATO being brought against it. If the Soviet Union were ever to think that the United States would not be ready to respond, then the free world would indeed be in danger. Finally, in the aftermath of Viet Nam, we must adapt ourselves especially in NATO to not think only in terms of protecting Europe directly. With the Soviet Union's access to warm-water ports and its navy spread around the world, the real danger in the immediate future, I submit, is not a frontal attack on Europe but the eating away of the free world's interests around the world wherever there is a soft underbelly, preferably by proxy. We have to make NATO a little bit quicker on its feet.

The United States and the European Community have a fundamental identity of views, interests, and values that must lead us to insure that the strategic requirements of interdependence dominate over the day-to-day practical tussles of national interests. In the same way that the future success of the European Community depends on the readiness of our governments to constantly extend the frontiers of interdependence, so too, in my view, the future of the values on which our western way of life depends is bound up with each other's fate in an increasingly closely knit and interdependent world. The ideals for which we stand are common to us both. Over centuries past they have made an imperishable contribution to human progress. And it is the duty of our generation, yours and mine, to see that they can continue to develop in strength and freedom. That must be our common aim, despite whatever differences there may appear to be between us in day-to-day matters. Let us never lose sight of that common aim.

Is Interdependence New or Important?
Robert Solomon

Is interdependence really new? Certainly the perception of interdependence, particularly in the United States, has intensified in recent years. Probably OPEC had a lot to do with our new sensitivity to other's actions, though the interdependence with OPEC is not exactly symmetrical. And perhaps the enormous rise in food prices throughout the world in 1972-73 also helped to heighten our perception of interdependence. But people who live in Europe have been consciously aware of interdependence for a long time.

Our measure of the long-lived nature of interdependence is revealed in the historical statistics pulled together very conveniently by Professor Simon Kuznets. They show that the ratio of international trade to total output in most industrial countries has been increasing, with one major interruption, since the beginning of the Industrial Revolution. Growing international trade relative to output is not a new phenomenon. But this tendency which went on through the eighteenth and nineteenth centuries stopped in 1913 with World War I. It resumed for a very brief period in the 1920s, again declined in the Great Depression of the 1930s, and resumed its climb only in the mid-1950s. So there was a period of roughly fifty years when the long-term tendency of trade to increase relative to output was interrupted.

Without this longer view of history, many people viewed the resumption in the mid-1950s of international trade growth as a new phenomenon. I am tempted to quote Santayana, who said (not in these precise words) that he who ignores history is condemned to relive it. To illustrate my point, two political scientists published an article in 1961 based on statistics for the period 1913-59, which demonstrated that Sombart's Law (of the decreasing importance of export trade) was in fact valid.[2] What they were doing was drawing conclusions from one segment of a long-term upward trend—the segment, alas, that happened to include a reversal of that trend.

More recently, trade has been increasing quite rapidly in relation to output. In the last ten years, exports of the United States have doubled as a percentage of its GNP, and if you relate trade to the output of only so-called tradable goods, it would be seen to have increased even more, both in recent years and over the longer time spans noted above. Today, U.S. exports are about 8 percent of its GNP.

For individual European countries, as we all know, trade is a much higher portion of output or GNP. But for the European Community as a whole, exports to the outside world seem to be only about 12 percent of the combined GNPs of member states. The remainder of their exports go to each other rather than to the outside world. The difference between the U.S. and European Community percentages, therefore, isn't all that great. The European Community as a group seems to be not much more open, so to speak, than the United States.

My main point is that the quantitative growth of trade relative to output, which is the phenomenon most often referred to when people speak of interdependence, is not a new development. But there have been qualitative changes in the nature of this interdependence. An increasing proportion of world trade in the period since World War II has been carried on among industrial countries, for example, and that is a new phenomenon. Kuznet's statistics show that for a long span of years the proportion of world trade accounted for by industrial countries was quite constant. But it has increased markedly since World War II, in good part, I suspect, because of rapid growth in intra-European trade.

Of course, other forms of international economic intercourse also have become increasingly important. Travel is a well-known example. When I was an undergraduate, I had one friend who had been to Europe: he was a very unusual person. These days, it is very difficult for a college student to have one friend who has not been to Europe.

Worker migration, both in Europe and in this hemisphere, to cite another example, has become a very important phenomenon. Workers migrate in both directions, sometimes returning home voluntarily, sometimes involuntarily when work permits are cancelled by host governments. For a while, direct investment was dominated by American investment abroad. Now we read in the newspapers everyday of a new European or Japanese investment in the United States. And movements of financial capital among nations have accelerated greatly in recent years.

All these forms of international economic intercourse are important aspects of international interdependence; they impact the economies of the countries involved in numerous ways. So, the answer to my first question, Is interdependence really new? is no. Interdependence is not a new phenomenon, but it has some new qualitative features, and, of course, the greater interdependence becomes, the greater probably both the benefits and costs become.

Let me then turn to the significance and the implications of the new interdependence. Interdependence, I suppose, means some form of mutual sensitivity among the countries of the world to each other's situation. Mutual vulnerability, even. Mutual exposure—exposure of one country to what is happening in other countries. And exposure to what is expected to happen in other countries. Expectations play a large role as well in the transmission of impulses from one country to another.

This interdependence brings benefits and costs, as I say. Sir Christopher Soames has pointed out very well that greater interdependence does bring increased welfare through greater specialization, economies of scale, and increased output. Travel, obviously, brings enrichment of lives and other benefits. And one can point out the benefits that still other forms of interdependence entail.

But interdependence also creates tensions, and there are various ways to express the problems that are created by the existence of interdependence. The simplest and shortest way to say it is that there is a clash between the political independence and economic interdependence of countries. From the economist's point of view, increased interdependence means that the autonomy of national policies is weakened. Countries still have policy instruments they can use. They can raise or lower taxes. They can increase or decrease government expenditures. They can use their monetary policies. They can engage in other types of economic policies. But the impact of those policies may be either blunted or accentuated by influences from abroad. So in a way, there is a clash between the real gains from interdependence and the achievement of domestic goals.

To illustrate the point, consider Germany and Japan this year. Both their currencies have appreciated, and the upward movement of the deutsche mark and the yen has implications for domestic economic policy in Germany and Japan. A second example is increased manufactured goods imports by developed countries from the more industrialized developing countries. This increase in manufactured imports certainly brings benefits to consumers in the importing nations: they like Brazilian shoes and Korean apparel compared to the alternatives at given prices. But these imports also bring unemployment problems to the importing nations, and they bring pressures for protectionism from trade unions and others.

Since most of us believe that the benefits of interdependence are important and should be preserved, the problem is to learn how to cope with the costs of interdependence; how to manage interdependence internationally.

One way to manage interdependence is to create some form of policy coordination, but the word *coordination* has more than one meaning. In Europe, particularly among members of the European "snake" (an arrangement to narrow the margins of fluctuations among member currencies), the word *coordination* tends to mean similarity—to coordinate policies, you adopt similar policies, particularly similar monetary policy. This is a necessary condition for the preservation of the poor snake, such as it is. But in the worldwide sense, the word *coordination* has to have a different meaning. It cannot mean that all countries should be adopting the same or similar policies. Rather, it means that countries need to take into account, when they adopt and formulate their own domestic policies, what is going on in the rest of the world. Countries have to try to make their policies compatible.

To solve these problems of interdependence, perhaps the most important requirement is what I would call empathy. Countries have to somehow see each other's points of view. Or, in the words of Sir Christopher, they have to get into each other's skin—not under each other's skin, which is an American expression for irritating somebody else—but *into* each other's skin. To be empathetic. To see the other country's point of view—a necessary but not a sufficient condition for dealing with interdependence.

Institutional Responses to the New Interdependence
Senator Alan Cranston

The international system has changed dramatically, particularly in the last thirty years. Interdependence is no longer just a choice for nations; it is a reality—at times a very harsh reality. It is a reality accentuated by an unprecedented increase in international communications, mobility, literacy; a reality fashioned by the breakup of old empires, the creation and participation of new nation-states, and in the international system, the clash of ideologies among states and by increased expectations; a reality underscored by the recognition and assertion of basic human rights.

Our nations, the industrialized democracies, have a common commitment to individual rights, to free societies based on the principles of liberty, democratic procedures, and mutual consent. Our independence is also based upon a concern for collective security and upon the realities of the international economic system (to the degree that we understand those realities). We are not fair-weather allies. We are lasting friends. We enjoy the privilege of living in free societies where it is safe to say unpopular things and to be unpopular. Even more important, while we have the freedom to choose from among a wide range of alternatives, we recognize that what we do will affect others. The old standard responses simply are not adequate to solve the problems created by new international realities.

In the 1970s, many of the nations of the world have had to cope with lingering, widespread inflation; severe balance of payments disequilibriums; a serious, persistent recession; and high unemployment from which we are slowly recovering. No single factor, of course, created these economic circumstances. They sprang from a combination of expansionary monetary and fiscal policies in the late sixties and the early seventies, increases in the prices of primary commodities, a fourfold rise in the price of oil, and the breakdown in the Bretton Woods system. These all came together, causing a demand for new solutions and approaches to a new configuration of problems.

The system today is characterized by an increasing interdependence among nations across issue areas. It requires greater international cooperation in the fields of food, energy, oceans, arms control, nuclear proliferation, and pollution—all matters transcending boundaries. Problems once considered to be domestic are no longer confined by the boundaries of nation-states. Similarly, the consequences of actions taken by individual nations are played out far beyond their national borders. Global problems need global approaches. Newcomers to the international system, especially, want to develop a greater level of national autonomy and are less willing to sacrifice what they consider to be their immediate well-being for more remote internationalist objectives. Even the United States has responded at times to global challenges in a very nationalistic manner.

To reap the benefits of interdependence, the nations of the world must devise ways to make interdependence work. International institutions and forums, such as the World Bank, the International Monetary Fund, the United Nations, the General Agreement on Tariffs and Trade (GATT), and NATO have played key roles in improving regional and global well-being. They responded to and even prevented some economic disruptions. They have been useful for improving communications, cooperation, and problem-solving. Certainly, some institutions have not worked as well as it was hoped, but, on the average, they have been essential components of the international system since we began to recover from World War II.

However, these institutions must be adapted to meet new requirements and new challenges. Specifically, I think we must enlarge participation in the international system to include both the newcomers and the "dropouts" wherever possible. To a large extent, the hopes and expectations of the developing world and the tensions in the North-South dialogue result from inadequate Third and Fourth World representation in existing international institutions and forums. The dropouts, that is, the nations of Eastern Europe, the Soviet Union, and the People's Republic of China, should participate when it is feasible for them to do so. We must realize that the economies of the East and West are increasingly interdependent.

Second, the industrialized democracies are in a position to encourage the use of functional institutions as the best forums for dealing with specific issues. Special trade problems could be addressed within the framework of GATT; the supply of commodities within the United National Conference on Trade and Development (UNCTAD), and debt problems within the Paris club.

Third, we must make existing international institutions more efficient and more responsive, and establish better means for informal collaboration at early stages before final agreements are reached on specific policies. This includes the task of facilitating greater coordination of institutional responses across issue lines. We should resist the bureaucratic phenomenon of many international institutions dealing concurrently with global issues such as energy, pollution, trade, and development assistance. Our resources are simply too scarce and our time too limited to be utilized in overlapping, redundant efforts.

Fourth, I believe we must increase each nation's willingness, as best we can, to participate more responsibly in the international system, whether through formal institutions, forums, conferences, or negotiations, as a means of approaching and resolving common problems. The new interdependence recognizes that there is no such thing, really, as a unilateral solution. Political leaders today are being asked to act in the larger national interest, to resist the short-run temptations to export domestic problems to other nations. To do otherwise promotes beggar-thy-neighbor practices that can tip the fragile balance we must preserve.

While our political leaders must realize that international cooperation is vital and in their own national interest, our international institutions have a responsibility to take into account the legitimate concerns of each nation and its people.

Finally, we must find new avenues for resolving some of our difficulties with the Soviet Union. The United States and the Soviet Union, with their allies, are in approximate strategic balance today. By looking beyond standard military indicators of power, however, the West's superiority in economic, technological, social, political, and human terms becomes very evident. I say this not in a spirit of boastfulness, but rather with a sense of sober responsibility that should lead to a realization of the unparalleled opportunity that is in our hands. For in this balance sheet, we of the West should find the self-confidence we need to lead the way to a more stable and secure era and to a gentler, a freer, and a more bountiful world.

Certainly, we must have no illusions about the serious differences between the aims of the Soviet Union and the West, or about the nature of the Soviet system. We should proceed from a recognition of the simple fact that the Soviet Union and the West have many, many competing and conflicting interests. Yet it is also in the interest of both sides to regulate their competition and conflict so that they do not lead to the dangers of nuclear war.

This long-term sense of common cause and destiny requires, in my judgment, our mutual engagement in the following endeavors:

1. More energetic and effective efforts by both sides to achieve agreements for the stabilization and reduction of the strategic military competition between the Soviet Union and the West. That is what Salt II is all about. Clearly, a military equilibrium is essential in today's world. But it is vital to the real security interests of all of us that this equilibrium be as stable and at as moderate a level as can be negotiated based not on trust (because frankly, we don't trust the Soviet Union and we know they don't trust us), but on verifiable agreements and concrete actions.

2. More effective and concerted efforts by all countries possessing nuclear capabilities to avert further proliferation of nuclear weapons.

3. Immediate negotiations to regulate the dangerous competition in conventional weapons and the literally insane scale of sale and transfer of such weapons from country to country all over the world.

4. Fresh initiatives on the part of the Soviet Union and the nations of the West to commit ourselves to greater mutual restraint in such present and potential conflict areas as Africa, the Middle East, the Indian Ocean, the Persian Gulf, and such other conflict situations as will surely arise in the time ahead.

5. The measured development of economic, commercial, social, cultural, and other forms of societal intercourse between the West and the Soviet Union, with due and deliberate regard for the balance of risks and advantages of such relations.

Notes

1. Richard N. Cooper, *The Economics of Interdependence,* p. 5. Reprinted with permission.

2. Karl W. Deutsch and Alexander Eckstein, "National Industrialization and the Declining Share of the International Economic Sector, 1890-1959," *World Politics* 13 (1961):267-99.

3 Europe at Nines and Twelves

Perhaps the most interesting example of international efforts to implement a strategy of cooperation and coordination is to be found in relations among member states of the European communities. For it is in Western Europe that we find the most dramatic metamorphosis of political and economic attitudes in recent times, from a condition of interstate suspicion and siege no more than a generation ago, to one of willing though as yet incomplete economic integration and significant concessions of sovereignty today.

A Vision of European Unity

By the end of World War II, the flames of battle had consumed thirty million Europeans, displaced sixteen million more who had been forced to flee their homelands, and destroyed many great cities of Europe. Berlin had lost nearly 75 percent of its buildings; Düsseldorf, Hamburg, and Frankfurt, even more. Central parts of London were wastelands. Industrial and agricultural production had shriveled by more than one-half, transportation networks had collapsed, and financial bankruptcy seemed imminent everywhere. The necessities of life were desperately short, and prospects for the future looked dim. Few Europeans believed that within their lifetime the fruit of European recovery would surpass the standards of living of prewar years.

Yet, phoenixlike, Europe rose again from its ashes. With the help of Marshall Plan aid, quickened saving and investment, and a remarkable vision of the advantages of European unity, the peoples of Europe achieved steadily higher real incomes to the point early in the seventies of near equality with those of Americans. They attained these generous living standards, moreover, not through hostile conquest of other nations or armed revolution, but by peaceful methods of organizing political and economic decisions which demanded common deliberation and assent. This chapter, including the conference remarks by Ambassador Spaak and Ranieri Bombassei, focuses especially on the methods of cooperation and coordination employed in the institutions of the European communities.

Many Europeans and some Americans made significant contributions to the task of building Western Europe's postwar institutions, but none is more properly credited with the title "Mr. Europe" than France's Jean Monnet. As early as World War I, when he helped to organize a joint Franco-British Supply Commission, Monnet dedicated his abundant energies to persuading European governments that they should reach beyond narrow national concerns to grasp common European interests. It was he, on the eve of the fall of France in June, 1940, who appealed to Churchill and de Gaulle to proclaim a Franco-British political union; and it was he, undaunted by French rejection of his plan in 1940, who inspired much of the postwar crusade to unite Europe.

His persistence bore fruit initially in the Schuman Plan to pool European coal and steel industries under a supranational high authority. Unlike the conception of the OEEC, which left the instruments of intergovernmental cooperation in the hands of member governments, the idea behind the Monnet-inspired Schuman Plan called for a governing structure that largely pooled decision-making authority in a central body, binding France, Germany, and other member countries to the outcome of high authority discussions. To be sure, this dramatic departure in the political and economic life of Europe was limited at first to a single industrial sector. Failure of the experiment would not, then, do the political damage that failure of a grander, more sweeping innovation would. But its success, by the same token, could smooth the way for other experiments, and ultimately, Monnet thought, it could lead to full political federation.

In the event, the European Coal and Steel Community was successfully ratified in 1951, when six European nations—Belgium, France, Germany, Italy, Luxembourg, and the Netherlands—signed the Paris treaty. The United Kingdom chose not to join, still preferring its vision of international cooperation to that of the limitations on sovereignty implicit in a high authority. It would be wrong, however, to infer from the United Kingdom's action that the parties to the Paris Treaty shared equivalent degrees of readiness to surrender political autonomy. Indeed, neither the attempt subsequently to establish a European Defense Community nor repeated efforts to set up a European political community were successful because each would have involved unacceptable abrogations of national power. Rather, the reason that some joined in the experiment and the United Kingdom did not was traceable to differing perceptions of the specific economic advantages to be gained by affiliation in the ECSC and to understandable differences among the nations of Europe in the strength of their expectations that economic integration would lead to less conflict, greater security, and strengthened political institutions. The United Kingdom was more doubting than others, and stayed out.

The European Communities

The new experiences of working together in the ECSC—and the regret of having failed narrowly to establish a common European defense com-

munity—emboldened the proponents of European unity to push on toward
more comprehensive methods of integration. Thus, planning for the European Economic Community and the European Atomic Energy Community
began in earnest at the conference of Messina in 1955, to which the member
governments of the ECSC gave their careful attention. And the United
Kingdom, eager to promote its alternate vision of European unity, proposed almost immediately the establishment of a free trade area for Western
Europe—a more widespread yet looser-knit commercial arrangement,
which like the EEC plan would remove restrictions on the movement of
goods and services among member countries, but which would not force
them to harmonize tariffs, quotas, or other restrictive devices on its trade
with nonparticipating countries. Nor did the United Kingdom's proposal
imply nearly so much intent to emerge someday with a politically federated
Europe. After examining both sets of proposals, the U.S. government threw
its primary support to the European Community's proposal, preferring at
this juncture the vision of a united Europe that held the greater potential for
eventual federation.

Ambassador Spaak's account of the achievements and prospects of the
European Community picks up at this point. The EEC (the Common
Market) and Euratom were established in 1957 with the signing of the treaty
of Rome by the six continuing members of the ECSC. Once again, the
United Kingdom stayed outside. The treaty itself, the Ambassador points
out, is mute about many of the common problems which, in later years,
have plagued the Community's members, forcing them to develop case-by-
case responses, some individually and some collectively, to such challenges
as energy, the environment, relations with developing countries, and
regional imbalances. But the Community's common institutions have made
it possible to respond imaginatively to the challenge of many common
needs, he avers, despite the fact that they are not, strictly speaking, institutions of government. Indeed, the story that he tells sounds remarkably like a
projection of Monnet's initial vision: That any group concerned with an international problem will be influenced by the structure within which it
works. As long as institutions are reasonably clear about the international
character of their purposes and are governed by agreed procedures, Monnet
forecasts, the people who work for and within such institutions will develop
instincts for shared solutions. Familiarity breeds respect for common efforts.

The institutions of which the ambassador speaks were modeled after
the successful ECSC institutions: an executive body, represented by the high
authority which formulated and proposed policies and implemented approved policies; a Council of Ministers that needed to approve all proposals
from the high authority and represented the interests of the national governments; a Parliamentary Assembly that oversaw the budget; and a Court of
Justice that adjudicated disputes arising out of high authority or member

state actions under the treaty. Initially, each community had separate executive bodies (or commissions, as they came to be called) and Councils of Ministers, while sharing in common the parliament and court. But by 1967, sufficient progress had been made in regularizing procedures so that a single commission and a single council took over the respective duties of multiple predecessor commissions and councils, in accordance with the rules specified in the three community treaties. These rules differed somewhat, leading to the anomaly that the balance of decision-making power under terms of the ECSC treaty rested with the Commission, while that of the EEC resided in the Council.

Ambassador Spaak speaks also, as did Sir Christopher Soames in the last chapter, of the growing power of external attraction of the Economic Community. Its magnetism developed first in the sixties. Unhampered by the narrow mandates of the ECSC and Euratom and buoyed by the ambitious goals of its own treaty, it prospered greatly during the period of most rapid economic growth in Europe, becoming by mid-decade the dominant economic force of Europe. It was about this time, he notes, that the Community also began to better identify its own interests, particularly within the framework of multilateral trade negotiations and in its relations with nations of the developing world. As a consequence of these trends, other nations of Europe found the lure irresistible and began, one by one, to explore the desirability of membership. Britain's initial overture in 1963 was rebuffed by President de Gaulle, as was its 1967 application for entry. But new initiatives carried Britain, Ireland, and Denmark into the Community in 1971, following the retirement of de Gaulle and the completion of intricate negotiations involving the Common Agricultural Policy, the independent funding of some Community activities, and planning for an economic and monetary union. Then they were nine.

The enlargement of the Community to nine members added new weight, as well as new problems, to the process of achieving European unity. Popular attitudes in two new member states were lukewarm or hostile to Community objectives. The referendum in Denmark that authorized accession had passed narrowly, even as a similar vote failed in Norway despite support of all major political parties. The British public also seemed negative, reflecting a general mistrust of the Community as well as the opposition by an important wing of the British Labour party and by parts of the Conservative party. These doubts have compromised the ability of any British government to operate effectively in the Community. The absorption of three new member states also raised a host of political and procedural problems which, in view of Ranieri Bombassei, delayed or set back the Community's momentum toward union. Simply dealing with three additional governments, their policies, and their bureaucratic politics vastly complicated the process of working out harmonious solutions to common problems.

Progress in further refining Community objectives was set back still further by dramatic external events early in the seventies. The energy crisis commencing in 1973 caught the Europeans wholly unaware and revealed through reactions in individual member states, as described by Ambassador Spaak, a seemingly shallow resolve to meet common crises collectively. The resulting uncertainty, followed by recession and virtual stagnation in all member countries, collapsed hope of making progress toward economic and monetary union, moreover, and even suggested that the objective previously set to achieve full union by 1980 might have been anchored more in "Eurocrats' " eagerness for new initiatives than in the reality of domestic political conditions in member states. Then, too, the realization that national inflation rates were diverging once again and that none was responding easily to traditional economic prescriptions, increased the possibility of member nations seeking alternative strategies that would improve their own inflationary or recessionary condition, but at the expense of partner countries. The potential for independent protectionist strategies definitely had risen.

New Initiatives

It may seem odd to the outside observer, therefore, that the latter part of the 1970s has witnessed three new and ambitious initiatives for further developing the Community. The first of these, the instituting of direct elections to the European Parliament, is explored in the next chapter with the special help of three distinguished parliamentarians from Britain, Holland, and Germany. The second initiative was the effort to revive progress toward economic and monetary union by creating at the beginning of 1979 a new European monetary system, including a new European unit of account and pooled reserves to back it; it is discussed in chapter 5. And the third—perhaps the most complex of all—is the further expansion of membership in the European Community (formerly the EEC) to include three applicants from the south of Europe: Greece, Portugal, and Spain. It is described later by Ranieri Bombassei.

The distinctive feature of all three developments is their defensiveness, which is to say they have been put forward within the Community as ways to preserve gains already achieved, rather than primarily as means to achieve further unity and ultimate federation. They are not easily seen, alternatively, as new versions of programs proposed in the middle and late sixties. The purpose of electoral reform of the European Parliament seems to be to stem the erosion of confidence by Europeans in the institutions of the European Community—to legitimize, as it were, the polity of the Community. The purpose of establishing a new European monetary system, by the same token, apparently is to guard the European economy against untoward side effects of dollar instability and to attain peculiarly domestic political objectives in at least the two largest member nations, Germany and France. And according to Mr. Bombassei, the primary motivation of the Nine in looking favorably upon the three Mediterranean applicants is to help assure the survival of their fledgling democratic governments. Otherwise, surely, the economic costs of assimilating these lesser developed European states would have proved much too high for accession.

That this new wave of change in the European Community has been produced from perceptions in member states that certain problems demand European solutions is highly encouraging. As noted in chapter 1, member states increasingly feel *restrictions* on their capacities to achieve domestic objectives and interests by acting unilaterally, and therefore they frequently acquiesce to international arrangements, such as the European communities provide, which are meant to relieve some restrictions. On questions such as threats to neighboring democratic institutions, fears of imported inflation or unemployment, and the legitimacy of parliamentary budgetary processes, there seems to have been sufficient coincidence of domestic objectives within the communities to justify pushing forward with these latterday reforms. But note, even so, that the impulse for fundamental reforms of these consequences probably must originate in the perceived interests of member state polities to make their success reasonably possible. The days of Eurocratic initiatives that succeed are much less frequent.

But it should also be noted that all three innovations are being used by member states as new *opportunities*, even while attesting to their willingness to cooperate with other nations, to sponsor their own private or governmental interests. In the case of direct elections to the European Parliament, for example, the French recently have taken positions in debates about how the parliamentary budget is to be funded, and about how and how much directly elected members of the European Parliament are to be paid, which are calculated to prevent the passage of additional supranational power to the Parliament. In a similar way, the French government at the beginning of 1979 took action to delay the introduction of the European Monetary System, planned for the beginning of the year, until it could extract a promise from its community partners to settle outstanding French complaints about common farm prices. German motives for having sponsored a new European monetary system in the first place, moreover, seem to have been linked to a newly found readiness to assume a leadership role in the foreign affairs of the Community, indeed, even of the world, despite what appear to be rather costly commitments to the success of the system. Negotiations between the European Community and three new applicant states—especially those with Spain—also are beginning to reveal new opportunities for member states to achieve national objectives that otherwise would have been difficult to attain; for example, regional assistance for the south of Italy and France.

Europe today appears to be standing at a turning point. It clearly has lost the romantic vision of political federation that Jean Monnet, in word and in deed, so eloquently projected for the postwar generation of Europeans. Its common institutions, especially those of the European Community, continue to serve the common purposes of member states, but without the compelling momentum and the almost euphoric sense of destiny that animated Community affairs in the early 1960s. Innovations still are possible, as direct elections, monetary initiatives, and enlargement discussions indicate, but they seem more and more the creations of national political forces than of a spirit of European unity. For each instance of optimism, as expressed by Ambassador Spaak, there seems a countervailing note of caution or warning, as voiced by Ranieri Bombassei. In reference to further expansion, he mentions that "the days when we could just muddle through for better or worse are over." If Europe cannot recapture a sense of collective destiny, the opportunity of coping with the new interdependence seems dim indeed.

Conference Highlights

Achievements and Prospects of the European Community
Ambassador Fernand Spaak

I'll look at the Community's achievements, then at its psychology. Third, I'll look at its prospects, which is to say the strengths of its internal purpose. And finally, I'll try to explain the external power of attraction of the Community.

Looking very superficially at the achievements of the Community, I see four main bases for developing our efforts toward further economic and political integration of Europe. The first is most important, yet we hardly talk about it anymore in Europe. It is the fact that war is no longer thinkable among the nine countries of the Community—not only military war, but also economic war. Thus, our second achievement is a new economic solidarity. We learned a lesson in the 1930s—that it doesn't pay to try to shift the burden of your economic problems onto your neighbor's shoulders. We are trying—I underline *trying*—to solve our problems together. The third achievement is our Common Market. We have a large economic area of 260 million consumers—300 million if we add Greece, Portugal, and Spain—consumers who can move freely in the Community and who can sell and buy goods that are produced in any of the nine countries, without any government restrictions. This is the sort of economic freedom that you have enjoyed in America.

The fourth achievement is the existence of common institutions. We have an executive branch, a legislative branch, and a judiciary branch of government. Of course, we are not a government; but we have been given the task of dealing with a number of government responsibilities. It is an essential asset of our present and necessary for our future to be able to count on common institutions and to feel that the trend of those institutions is toward further and further democratization. The fact that the European Parliament will be directly elected next year is a sign of this trend.

We have been helped in our achievements by a very simple fact of Europe: that most of the economic or social problems we face are problems that we no longer can solve individually or as single nations. Individually we are too small to be effective.

Once we have recognized this fact, we are bound to work for common European solutions. Agriculture and industry—the industry of tomorrow, such as aerospace and electronic equipment; as well as the industry of yesterday, such as steel, textiles, and shipbuilding—cannot be solved alone. We can no longer really improve workers' conditions without taking a common European view of the problem. The problems of environment, the problems of conserving fish stocks in Community waters, and our relationships with the developing and the industrialized worlds, are issues that no longer can be viewed from a purely national perspective. Faced with these numerous challenges, what has the Community done?

I like to characterize the present state of the Community's development as one of gradually growing out of adolescence. The Community is becoming an adult. It still shows signs of great youth. It still has the adolescent uncertainties. For instance, it lacks confidence in itself, confidence in the strength of its capacity to solve its own problems. Faced with a problem such as unemployment which is common to all the countries of Europe, for example, the Community is just beginning to recognize that it will only be solved by moving toward economic and monetary union. Perhaps the medicine has been too strong to take. The Community also behaves like an adolescent when faced with sudden emergencies. It sometimes has unduly brash attitudes toward outside countries, including Third World nations. It also suffers from high fever sometimes. We have a tendency when we meet with an obstacle to talk immediately of disruption of the Community, of betrayal of ideals, of treason. This, of course, is also a sign of youth. As a matter of fact, we haven't quite gotten used to the difficulty of living together. This explains the impatience that is sometimes felt by our partners in the rest of the world. Faced with a community that finds it very difficult to make up its mind, other nations are often puzzled when, after agreement, the Community acts with a sort of impulsiveness, even brutality at times. But the failures of the Community have been the paving stones of our progress, and we have been strengthened rather than weakened by the failures we have known in the past twenty-five years. The Community is coming of age.

The sign of its greater maturity grows with a greater sense of responsibility. It is very striking to notice that we are gradually moving out of the limitations of the initial, basic treaties of Paris and Rome. Using the tools that we have been provided with—institutions, financial interventions, a budget—we are gradually undertaking tasks that were unheard of twenty-five years ago. Who would have thought about an environment policy fifteen or twenty-five years ago? Yet without any reference to it in the basic treaties, the Community is developing an environment policy and is making decisions on environmental laws enforceable in the nine countries.

Nor did we mention the possibility of an energy policy in 1952, despite our long-term awareness of the problems of coal. And yet, the implementation of an energy policy that will be common to the Nine is today one of the main economic objectives of the Community. A regional policy, which has become one of the conditions of further progress toward economic and monetary union, was not mentioned in the treaties. Nevertheless, there are now regional funds in the Community, enabling transfers to be made from the richer to the poorer parts of the Community—insufficient certainly, but ready to be used in more intensive ways. We also are coming of age in the field of external relations. That is to say, we can identify our own interests and define our policies. And we have the institutions to give the Community a will and the means to achieve its own purposes. But also, and mainly, we are finding out that every year brings to the Community a greater wealth of experience, on the basis of which we can build further.

President Jenkins closed his recent State of the Union message to Parliament with the comment: "Let the strength of our internal purpose be at least as great as our external powers of attraction." To be very candid, the strength of our internal purpose is perhaps our weakest area of development. Before 1973-74, we thought that by 1980 we would have an economic and monetary union. We could see the various stages that would lead us to this most important achievement. Then the energy crisis occurred in 1973, at a time when we were importing more than 95 percent of our oil from the OPEC countries. The impact of the embargo and of oil price increases was of dramatic importance to our economy and to our cohesion as a Community. We did not meet that challenge very brilliantly. We thought initially that we might better deal with the energy crisis by scrambling for safety—under the illusion that national banners would best protect our interests. It took the Arab nations to tell us that this was not so and that they were no longer interested in a dialogue with single European countries.

What they wanted as a partner in the discussions that started in 1973 was a community, a community of 260 million consumers. We understood the lesson, but perhaps a little too late to avoid the psychological impact of our failure to remain together during this very serious crisis.

At the same time that higher energy prices were felt, inflation started raging and unemployment started rising in the Community. There again, we failed to tackle those problems together. We didn't yet have the same social and economic priorities that would have made common economic policies possible. Some of our countries thought that the first priority was to safeguard employment, even at the cost of risking more inflation. Others thought that the greater risk for their economies was inflation, even if fighting inflation meant accepting a certain level of unemployment. The economic performances of the nine countries started diverging as they pursued different priorities. The target date of 1980 for economic and monetary union became utopian, and we forgot about it.

We forgot about it until the fall of 1977, when suddenly a new awareness arose, an awareness that we had been unable to solve the most important problems of our economies. Unemployment was still rising. The recession was lingering on, in spite of national efforts. We had to admit to ourselves that something had gone wrong, that the sometimes imaginative devices developed on a national basis did not meet the purpose. Now you hear people saying in various European capitals that even the most important national governments are no longer able to deal with unemployment and inflation without some sort of European Community framework. This has led the Commission to give life once again to the goal of economic and monetary union. We have now seen that it is a necessary condition to solving our fundamental economic problems of today and tomorrow.

We do 40 percent of world trade. For our countries, this represents on the average 25 percent of the gross national product, and of that amount, half is international trade among member countries of the Community. In other words, we are each other's most important economic partner. Even so, erratic fluctuations in the rates of currency exchange have become a tremendous obstacle to the further development of trade and investments among Community countries. Such fluctuations explain why we now feel that progress toward the solution of our economic problems requires that we do something about our currencies.

How do we foresee the next few years in terms of economic development? First, we do not believe that it is possible to move directly from the state in which we are today—that is, of more or less coordinated national policies—to full integration and a common set of economic policies. We believe that there will have to be intermediate steps, including intensified coordination of our economic policies and a more systematic look at monetary and budgetary policies. We first must try to reach common guidelines which will lead our governments toward development of consistent national policies.

Second, we feel that the time has come to strengthen our Common Market and change it into a single market. The Common Market is a customs union. Member governments have given up the possibility of interfering with trade within the union. We need to go further. We need to organize our market so that it will be just like the market of a single country. In other words, business activity must be developed within a common legal environment. Safety standards, for example, which are still different among member countries, will be harmonized. Only then will business firms be able to develop new investments with the view of a single market, facing not several but only one set of safety regulations. This, of course, will provide a further element of solidarity between our economies.

Yet another line of approach is to look at our problems of industrial structure. The years of recession have shown us that, in spite of the years of great prosperity in the sixties and early seventies, problems have arisen in some industries of the Community; in particular, steel, textiles, and shipbuilding. These problems can no longer be dealt with on a national basis, not only because we have a Common Market, but also because we face common problems of relations with the Third World. Our textiles problem, for instance, is closely linked with the policy the Community has developed toward the developing countries. It is also closely linked to the positions the Community is taking in multilateral trade negotiations. Also, for obvious reasons, readjustments in our industries will have to take into account our new concerns about the optimal manner of distributing Community resources—a manner much more intensive than was ever necessary at the national level.

But we are not dealing just with old industries. Aerospace and electronic components are high-technology industries that are developing in the Community much later than in the United States. Perhaps it is because the Common Market is so young that we waited so long to recognize the feasibility of investing in these capital-intense industries. Whatever the reason, we are now finding it difficult to establish their optimal sizes, even as they are confronted with very powerful American competitors.

Another example of the coming to maturity of the Community is our readjustment of the Common Agricultural Policy. In America, our agricultural policy is often criticized as being protectionist. Yet we consider ourselves to be a community of agricultural goods importers. In fact, our deficit in agricultural goods trade with the United States in 1977 was something like six billion dollars, quite a deficit for a Community that is considered protectionist. The fact that we are now importers of food and shall remain so gives greater importance to three elements of our policy. First, there is the need to assure availability of a minimum supply of food products. Second, we need to guarantee that food products will be available at reasonable prices. And third, we must guarantee our farmers a minimum standard of living. Now this has been achieved. The last fifteen years of our Common Agricultural Policy have shown that in spite of market fluctuations, necessary food was available in the Community at reasonable prices, though at somewhat higher prices than those available on the world market; Community farm prices were more stable than those on the world market, moreover, and sometimes even lower than those on the world market.

But we are now confronted with a new set of problems. The type of policy I have described has led to several structural improvements in the farming industry. We have reduced the number of farmers by half. We have enlarged the average acreage of farms in the Community. These developments have led to improved productivity of agriculture, leading to a tremendous increase in the production of agricultural products. We are running an enormous surplus of dairy products; for example, nonfat dry milk and butter are in great surplus in the Community. As a consequence, we have come to the point where we feel that we have to change our agricultural policy. We have to use the price mechanism to convince farmers to shift to other types of products. In the last two years, we have deliberately kept the prices of dairy products in particular at a lower level than the inflation rate. In other words, dairy farmers in the Community now are getting less money for their products in real terms than they got two years ago. This is a rather daring policy, but also a sign of the coming of age of the Community.

The last point of domestic policy to mention is our environment policy. In spite of the nonexistence of the word *environment* in our treaties, we have felt compelled to develop a policy in this field. Our environment policy deals with the sort of problems that are familiar to people in the United States. We have dealt with many decisions at the Community level concerning water management, the impact of chemicals on the environment, nature conservation, and noise abatement. When tackling those issues which are of immediate concern to our citizens, we also have the political development of Europe in mind. We are aware that next year our citizens will go to the polls to elect a candidate to the European Parliament. To make this election interesting to them, we have to provide them not only with answers, but also with at least several options that will guide the tasks of the future European Parliament.

My final remarks address our external power of attraction. I would like to outline the reasons why we have become another pole of attraction. The first, of course, is the strength of the Community as such. The fact is, over 260 million consumers constitute the largest market in the Western world, a very rich group of countries indeed. Our combined GNP is nearly the equivalent of the American gross national product. Our importance in the fields of trade and aid is even greater. Thus, the Community is an attraction simply because of its size. But also, the Community has been able to identify its interests as a community. It is quite remarkable that nine countries have been able to find out that their interests in the field of foreign relations are not only similar, but also could lead to common policies. Let me give two examples. The first is our relationship to the developing world. There is now in the Community a common feeling of responsibility for the development of countries linked to the Community by association agreements or the Lomé Convention. We have become aware that we face the same sort of problems, that we need their raw materials, and that in the future we will need their markets. It seems easy to have come to that conclusion, but it is quite remarkable that it has led to common policies. In our relationship with the industrialized world, we have developed a common awareness that our prosperity is linked to free trade. Once again, it seems perhaps more evident today than it was two or three years ago. France was not traditionally a free trade country. Nevertheless, it is now a member of the Community and shares the same awareness of our dependence on free international trade as countries more traditionally oriented to free trade, such as Britain or Germany.

On the basis of this awareness of common interests, we have been able to develop common policies toward the Third World, policies that represent a new approach affirming equal partnership with the developing world. Our new interdependence with the Third World is not based exclusively on facts, but rather, to a considerable extent it is an act of will on the part of the Community and its partners in the developing world. And toward the industrialized world, we have developed a common policy that has made the Community one of the most important partners in the now ongoing multilateral trade negotiations in Geneva. In fact, it has become obvious that in some international economic areas, the partnership between the United States and the Community is a condition for success. If we do not agree on what is to be done about international trade, there will be no success in the multilateral trade negotiations. If we do not agree on what has to be done toward the developing world, we will most probably be faced with international economic chaos in the future.

And finally, we have institutions that are able to put these policies into practice, institutions that are run by democratic principles, and institutions that have turned out to be valid partners. Indeed, the Community as an institution was fully represented at the London "summit" in May 1977, along with leaders from Japan, the United States, Canada, and several member governments of the Community. At the conference that took place in Paris between the developing world and the industrialized countries, again the Community and its institutions were present and acted as partners with the other industrialized countries. In other words, we have proved in the last few years that not only are we able to see our interests and to define our policies, but we are also competent to carry on the type of political activity required of governmental activity and responsibility.

The enlargement of the Community certainly can be regarded as another sign of the reality of the Community and its growing prospects. We felt very encouraged in 1973 when Britain, Ireland, and Denmark joined the initial six; it was a sign that we had suceeded in what we were attempting to do. The fact that last year three additional countries asked for membership in the Community is yet another sign of success. It is notable that these three countries—Greece, Portugal, and Spain—having just emerged from totalitarian regimes, took as their first act of democratic sovereignty requests to join the Community. They took these actions not only to enjoy the economic benefits of the Community, but also to give the strongest support possible to the democratic forces of their countries. Their actions show that the Community is indeed relevant to the problems of this world.

The Opportunities and Perils
of Enlargement
Ranieri Bombassei

One of the instructions of the preamble to the treaty of Rome is that only countries which are both European and democratic can become members of the Community. The proposed enlargement of the European Community to include Greece, Portugal, and Spain is a clear expression of the consequence of this doctrine. Once democracy had been restored in these countries, the doors of the Community opened. One of the first actions of each of their elected governments was to apply for membership in the Community, and in each case, the answer given by the Community's Council of Ministers was positive.

The motivation of the Council of Ministers in each case was overwhelmingly political, far more so than economic. Thus, if the problem of enlargement is primarily that of negotiating the economic conditions of accession, this can only be done in a way that will not endanger the political objective of enrollment in the European Community, namely, the political and economic integration of Europe. Such an objective poses problems that go far beyond those of accession to a simple customs union or free trade area. The question, then, is: What kind of Community should exist? The answer should be clear. We want a strong and coherent Community, aiming and marching toward economic and monetary union and European union. Seen in this light, the problem becomes quite clear, but the difficulties attached to its creation must not be underestimated. Only a clear understanding of the difficulties lying in the way of accession will allow us to overcome them.

Obfuscation of the real issues would merely lay hidden traps, both political and economic, for the Community on the path toward the goals it has set for itself.

In the first place, economic conditions are extremely unfavorable, far more so than during the previous enlargement of the Community. After an unprecedented period of prosperity and full employment which lasted into the early seventies, the whole economic fabric of the Western world was shaken by the monetary crisis, the rise in oil prices, and the consequent very strong recession—a recession that can be compared in its severity and duration to the Great Depression of the 1930s. None of our economies has yet fully recovered. If the Community has survived this major crisis, it has done so only by a holding operation and at the cost of further progress. All the more so, since during this period it has had to accomplish the proper integration of three new members—Great Britain, Ireland, and Denmark—who were not the least affected by the economic crisis.

The main area where the Community made some progress was in the field of external relations. But, here again, there is a limit to what more can be achieved without further internal progress. If the new challenge posed by the accession of three Mediterranean countries is not successfully met, there is a serious risk that the Community's credibility will be severely damaged, especially in the eyes of certain Asian and African countries, whose GNP is similar to Portugal's. The Community has guaranteed access to its market for a series of products, such as textiles, from these countries. Those products present considerable internal difficulty for the Community.

In the second place, Spain, like Greece and Portugal, is both less developed and less evenly developed than the existing member countries. Furthermore, all three are situated on the southern periphery of the Community, and this creates additional problems for the Community. It must be remembered, on the one hand, that the Community was created by countries principally in northern and central Europe, and thus certain changes have to be brought about to take into account the economies of countries situated in southern Europe. This is particularly important in the case of the Common Agricultural Policy, where certain past mistakes should be avoided, while ensuring a proper balance of advantages between farmers in the South and their brothers in the North. Not only in agriculture, but also in other fundamental sectors, such as regional and social policy, a better balance among less-favored and most-favored regions in the Community should be obtained. On the other hand, because they are less developed, regions in the South may find it difficult to live with existing regulations and follow the Community's policies now in force or under development.

Thus, unless something is done, the prime objective of strengthening the Community could be endangered. Rather than a stronger Community, a weaker one might result because of enlargement. To prevent this from happening, it seems that the best way to proceed is to ensure that the Spanish economy, as well as the economies of Greece and Portugal, develop more rapidly than the Community as a whole. This is the only way to progressively narrow the gap between these countries and the Nine. Given the balance of payments problems which, to varying degrees, all three have, this can only be done either by substantially transferring Community resources to these countries, or alternatively, by letting market forces operate. The Common Market represents close to 50 percent of their global export markets. In the past, this alone has insured a very fast rate of development of their economies, but in many cases it has led to heavy investments in sectors that are particularly sensitive in the Community, such as textiles, shoes, and shipbuilding. There is already a movement afoot to provide special protection for the Nine before imports from the three new members will be permitted. This situation shows well the difficulties of making way in the still economically vulnerable Community for candidates with specific problems of development.

The Community has to decide fairly quickly which road to follow: to allow the full play of market forces, a policy that would risk causing additional problems, not only at home, but also in relations with the developing world, thus necessitating a reassessment of certain aspects of Community trade policy; or to redirect production in the three countries, a policy that would require a very large transfer of resources; or both. Inevitably, whatever decision is taken on these courses of action, a much closer coordination of economic policies within the Community will be needed. It is a must. In addition, existing means of transferring resources within the Community will have to be strengthened and new means developed.

The corollary of this assertion is, of course, that in the future there will be two areas of Community policy, more or less dormant in the recent past, whose development in the complex of accession is vital. These areas are, first, economic and monetary union, and second, institutional improvements. Far from being a mirage that recedes ever further with the enlargement of the Community, economic and monetary union is one of the keys to overcoming the problems caused by a new enlargement. Without such progress, there is a likelihood that the gap between richer and poorer members of the enlarged Community will grow even wider, with consequent disastrous effects on internal cohesion even in established areas of Community policy. Wider economic disparities would seriously alter approaches to the future of the Common Agricultural Policy, to industrial policies, and to distribution of resources within the Community, including   regional policy.

With respect to institutional improvements, the experience of the previous enlargement has already made abundantly clear the difficulties attached to decision-making in the Community as it is today. A further increase in the number of member states to twelve risks paralysis of the already creaky Community decision-making machinery. There is no real alternative to a thorough overhaul of this machinery in the context of enlargement if the Community is to survive as a cohesive entity and not become an economic dinosaur. In its 1970 opinion about enlargement of the Community—an opinion that went deeply into these very questions—the Commission made clear its philosophy that the sine qua non of enlargement should be a strengthened Community. The reasoning that led the Commission to adopt that line is not out-of-date. Indeed, it has been proved right by experience, and the need for such an approach is even greater now than in the past. Since the Commission presented that opinion in 1970, the Community has increased to nine members. Completion and enlargement have been carried out. But strengthening has been forgotten. Perhaps the Community would have navigated more surely amid the perils of the last few years if it had been remembered.

This time, facing enlargement of a different nature, the Community cannot afford to take the same course. The necessary strengthening of the Community must take place parallel with enlargement. The days when we could just muddle through for better or worse are over. If we cannot comprehend and react to this new situation, then inevitably an enlarged Community will mean a diluted Community, a Community that falls far short not only of the visions of those who set it up, but also of the perhaps more pragmatic, but still optimistic ideas, of those who are involved with the development of the Community today. Neither the Nine nor the acceding states want such a diluted Community.

Postscript on Greece's Accession

After years of tedious negotiations, representatives of Greece and the European Community signed Greece's treaty of accession to the Community on May 28, 1979. The product of a carefully constructed compromise concerning the social and agricultural sectors, the treaty calls for formal accession at the beginning of 1981, but provides for a five-year period of transition for most Greek agricultural products and a seven-year transition for the free movement of Greek workers into Community member states.

This cautious and lengthy process of integration illustrates the delicacy of enlarging the Community under present circumstances. Of the three applicant countries, Greece clearly presented the easiest decision for the Community. It is already linked to the Community as an "associate" country, based on the agreement arranged by the Community with Greece in 1962. Under its terms, import duties already have been abolished for most Greek exports to the Community and for more than two-thirds of the Community's industrial exports to Greece; the remaining Greek barriers to

Community industrial goods already have been scheduled to be phased out during the next few years. Its agricultural exports to the Community, with the notable exception of peaches and tomatoes, impose relatively weaker threats to the livelihood of French and Italian farmers than do the exportable crops of Spain and Portugal. And its workers seem much less likely than those of Portugal to emigrate in large numbers to northern labor markets.

Yet the treaty of accession severely limits the potential economic effects of even these seemingly surmountable dislocations by stretching out the period of required adjustment—adjustment especially to higher agricultural prices in Greece and to modest shifts in the patterns of agricultural production in the Community's south. Thus, the treaty illustrates two important problems of enlargement spelled out by Ranieri Bombassei in the preceding contribution. Economically, it seems to show that the "costs" of dislocating particular producers and markets, at least in the short run, are perceived by the Community as exceeding the benefits of improved resource allocation through heightened market integration. Apparently, the gains from greater specialization, especially in the agricultural sector, either are not expected to come into being in sufficient magnitude to warrant imposing the costs or, more likely, are expected to be so widely (and therefore, weakly) shared by the consuming public that no effective advocate for freer trade through enlargement can be counted on to countervail the protectionist sentiments of particular interests. In either case, the lengthy period of adjustment called for by the treaty will provide extra time to engineer required shifts of resources, no doubt with the help of Community budgetary transfers to injured French and Italian farmers.

By the same token, the treaty also illustrates the political difficulties facing negotiations between the Community and the other two applicant states. Neither Spain nor Portugal has enjoyed associate status in the Community, as has Greece, and neither, therefore, is as far along as Greece in negotiating reciprocal reductions in import and export barriers. Spanish and Portuguese farm produce, moreover, is concentrated in Mediterranean goods such as wine, peaches, olive oil, apples, and tobacco, which compete directly with French and Italian agriculture; since Mediterranean goods now are sold in Spain at prices up to 60 percent cheaper than inside the Community, France is especially fearful that the entry of Spain could bankrupt many of its poorest farmers in the south. The prospects for Spanish and Portuguese accession are much less certain also because the very size of Spain means that the problems are relatively bigger, and because Portugal's economy is so weak. Then, too, enlargement to include Spain and Portugal would complicate even further the problem of achieving agreement in a system where most decisions have to be unanimous, including, it should be noted, decisions about the distribution of the regional and social funds. In short, Greece's accession to the European Community may prove to be one of a kind, at least for the remainder of the 1980s.

Direct Elections to the European Parliament

Measures of Legitimacy

Of the three most recent Community initiatives that were mentioned in the last chapter, direct election to the European Parliament seems, on first glance, to be the least likely to generate fundamental reform in the ways Community institutions respond to the challenge of the new interdependence. The treaty of Rome which established the Parliament (originally called the assembly) granted it very limited powers, and the 1976 action authorizing direct election of its members did not extend its powers significantly. The power of legislative initiative remains divided between the Commission, representing Community-wide interests, and the Council of Ministers, representing the national governments. On substantive policy proposals, to be sure, the Commission is obligated under the Rome treaty to consult the Parliament before taking them to the Council for approval, but the Parliament's role in these matters is more inquisitive than deliberative. Parliamentary control of the executive branch, in addition, continues to be limited in Community matters to the dubious right to remove the Commission by censure motion, and to its (not inconsiderable) influence over final approval of the Commission budget. Thus, to an American observer trained to appraise legislative power in congressional terms, the European Parliament appears weak and passive, direct elections notwithstanding.

The core of the Community's legislative process, by contrast, is guarded by the Council of Ministers which must approve proposals of the Commission before they can be implemented. Except in a very few cases, however, the Council cannot initiate proposals, but rather, must wait for the Commission to do so as outlined in the treaties of Rome. This means that the outcome of policy deliberations depends primarily upon the ability of the Commission and the Council—rather than the Parliament—to reach agreement on needed changes in policy. If the Commission does not propose changes, the Council is handcuffed; and if the Commission's proposals do not, in the Council's eyes, properly advance the common interest and do so without doing serious injury to particular national interests, they will fail to be approved.

Though the power to control agenda and the powers of bureaucratic continuity strengthen the Commission's hand in legislative negotiations with the Council, the balance of legislative power today no doubt rests with the Council of Ministers. This is true for several reasons: The Council does, after all, have the last word. It speaks with the authority of national interests, moreover, which in today's Europe is the dominant force shaping a response to the processes of internationalization. And the Council, alone among the institutions of the European Community, carries out its duties in much the same manner as the democratic institutions of Europe traditionally have functioned.

The European Community's main direct link with the people of Europe is through the Council. Although the members of the European Parliament until recently were appointed by virtue of their election to national parliaments, they are organized to do their work by party groupings rather than by national interest. Nor has their role in the development of the Community been a subject of public scrutiny or debate until recently. The pulse of the Commission is even more remote from the grasp of the people. The thirteen Commission members are appointed by agreement among the member governments, but are pledged to act in full independence of both their home governments and the Council. The Commission staffs, the Eurocrats, seem to have lost their nationalities altogether. Thus the absence of direct participation by the people of Europe in the affairs of the Community—except in the case of the Council of Ministers—has been both an explanation of the relative power of the Council and a symptom of the Community's failure to develop greater autonomy.

There were proposals to directly elect a European parliament as early as discussions leading to the creation of the European Coal and Steel Community, but member states showed little interest in direct elections until the mid-seventies. The reasons seem clear enough: National governments wanted to control the pace of European integration. As long as Europe-wide institutions lacked full legitimacy—which is to say that they could not claim to represent the people—democratically elected national governments doubted that European institutions could seize powers they did not want them to have. France's repeated uses of its Community membership to achieve national foreign policy objectives probably is the best example: A more autonomous Community would not have allowed France to manipulate Community actions to the extent that it has, for the purpose of enhancing its own international importance. Then, too, even pro-Community governments often hesitated to allow domestic elections to be dominated by the issues of Community rights and powers, lest more important domestic issues be lost in the tumult of debates over "supranationalism."

Structural Weaknesses

Why, then, did the Community decide on September 20, 1976 to move toward the direct election of the European Parliament? The decision does not appear to be the product of a single force. One force recommending the change was frustration over the state of the parliamentary process. Members of Parliament sat in two parliaments simultaneously—the legislative body of their home nation and the European Parliament. This fact produced several problems, including incompleted work, divided loyalties, and jet lag. Most proposals on direct elections stipulated that successful candidates could not serve also in a national legislature. The parliamentary process seemed awkward also to a growing body of influential Europeans whose service in one or another of the Community institutions had persuaded them that the strengthening of such institutions, including the Parliament especially, was a sine qua non of further progress toward solving some of Europe's most intractable common problems. Symbolic of this group were the many ''anti-Market'' parliamentarians who had developed understanding for the Community after serving in the European Parliament. For them and for the Eurocrats on the Commission and Council staffs, the European Community had become too important not to have more direct links with its public.

Thus, the motivation for direct elections was both defensive and hopeful. Having failed earlier in the decade to meet the energy crisis, make progress toward economic and monetary union, and harmonize foreign policies, European leaders, no matter how sympathetic they were to the goals of European federation, felt that precipitous steps toward further integration would be unworkable. Instead, they opted for a reform that at least initially would have no direct constitutional ramifications and would not upset the delicate balance between national and supranational power. Yet the desire for public participation in European Community affairs indirectly implied much more. For many, the common presumption concerning direct elections is that they will popularize the European Community and strengthen its autonomy by legitimizing another of its key institutions. Thus, on further reflection, the initiative that led to a directly elected European Parliament on June 7, 1979, may turn out to be the most important of the innovations mentioned in the last chapter. Time will tell.

The conference highlights of this chapter feature three distinguished European parliamentarians commenting on the subject of direct elections. Dr. Schelto Patijn is a laborite member of the Dutch and European parliaments; Dr. Martin Bangemann is a liberal member of the German and

European parliaments; and Mr. David Marquand, formerly a laborite member of the British parliament, at the time of the conference was liaison officer to the European Parliament for the Commission of the European Community. Their remarks are organized around three leading questions which promise to generate lively debate for years to come. They are: How will European politics be affected by directly electing the European Parliament? What kinds of relations will develop between national parliaments and the European Parliament? Will direct elections permit the European Parliament to gain power within the European Community?

The Politics of Direct Elections

To better appreciate the nature of conference disagreements on questions of politics, the reader needs to know that European politics by and large have two dominant features: party organization and national orientation. Party structure varies considerably from country to country in Europe, but it is significantly stronger everywhere in Europe than it is in the United States. Although all European states have a Labor party, a Liberal party, a Conservative or Christian Democratic party, and a Communist party, there has been relatively little intraparty cooperation across national boundaries. Political struggles among parties have been fought on a national level, for the most part, and "European" issues have rarely been discussed publicly on their merits.

Direct elections to the European Parliament will force change in these alignments. Since representatives will no longer be elected as Germans or Frenchmen—but instead, as socialists or liberals—European-wide political parties have had to be organized. As Dr. Bangemann notes, all parties now have adopted serious European programs. How will these European parties relate to their national counterparts? Will they always be "weak sisters"? Can national parties learn to work for common goals across European borders? It is hard to imagine an immediate shift away from nationally oriented party politics. Yet these international party institutions sooner or later will change the nature of European party politics.

One key to understanding the relation between national and European parties is the relation between national and European parliaments. Parliamentarians such as Dr. Patijn argue that the "double mandate" is unworkable and that the European Parliament must have its own corps of legislators that is not distracted by other legislative responsibilities. Others, such as Dr. Bangemann, feel that a double mandate would be a useful transitional device to keep national parliaments informed of developments in the Community; a separate group of European parliamentarians, he fears, will bring conflict with national institutions and thereby damage development of a healthy Community. A related issue: Can sufficient talent be recruited to adequately staff both the European Parliament and a full set of national legislatures? And still another issue: Will national parliaments, which after all are the embodiment of national sovereignty, be more or less likely to grant additional powers to the Community now that the European Parliament has become directly elected? Indeed, will the European Parliament still be contented with merely an advisory role to the Commission?

With respect to the Community's institutional structure, Sir Christopher Soames chided the parliamentarians for behaving too tamely in the past, and challenged them to seize their historic opportunity. "No parliament has ever gotten power without grabbing it," he said. Also Mr. Marquand felt that the Parliament must take a more aggressive stance toward both the Commission and the Council of Ministers. But the continental representatives did not agree. They argued that changes must occur slowly and organically. Dr. Patijn even guessed that little change will occur until a second election is held in the early eighties.

These differences in view between English and continental parliamentarians reflect historically significant differences in the ways their countries have organized government. Governance on the Continent is at once more consensual and more nonpartisan than in Great Britain. The fun of the democratic game as the English have played it for two centuries does not have a continental counterpart. Indeed, each member state has its own parliamentary traditions which no doubt will color the behavior in Strasbourg of most newly elected members of the European Parliament. It is only with the passage of time that "European" experiences will produce distinctively European parliamentary behavior; incremental changes in behavior are all that should be expected for a while.

Many conference speakers spoke of the imperatives of the new interdependence, of the commanding head start the process of internationalization has stolen on the polities of nations. Yet to those who study political developments, the abilities of political systems to adjust to interdependence seem so weak. The predominance of nationally oriented political concerns, growing regionalism in the West, and strident nationalism in the developing worlds all suggest that there will be less likelihood of greater cooperative efforts in the future than there has been in the past. At least at this moment in time, world trends seem to discourage the kind of political interdependence that the European Community symbolizes.

Even so, we are reminded by Jean Monnet, the father of the Community, how easy it is to confuse the difficulties of creating new institutional structures with the failure to make progress toward the goals of integration:

> Nothing would be more dangerous than to regard difficulties as failures . . . The roots of the Community are strong now, and deep in the soil of Europe. They have survived some hard seasons, and can survive

> more. On the surface, appearances change. In a quarter century, naturally, new generations arise, with new ambitions; images of the past disappear; the balance of the world is altered. Yet amid this changing scenery the European idea goes on; and no one seeing it, seeing how stable the Community institutions are, can doubt that this is a deep and powerful movement on a historic scale.[1]

By changing the nature of the European Parliament, decision-makers in Europe seem to have strengthened an institution that potentially represents greater political interdependence. If directly electing the European Parliament forces additional changes in the nature of domestic European politics, then the outlook for a strategy of coordination and cooperation may be made brighter.

Conference Highlights

An Overview of the European Parliament
Schelto Patijn

Where does the Parliament stand in the institutional structure of the European Community? The executive body—the Commission—makes proposals; the Council of Ministers establishes policy; and the Court of Justice monitors execution of the policies. Between the Commission and the Council is the European Parliament. Its normal functions are purely advisory. But it has one important task: it must approve the Community budget.

The budget power has given the Parliament leverage. The Community's rather big budget of $35 billion is decided upon, signed into law, and amended by the Parliament. Through a long struggle with the Council of Ministers, the Parliament achieved its preeminence. Budgetary power also provides the means to control the activities of the Commission. The parliamentary committees question commissioners about current business in closed meetings and at parliamentary sessions. The Parliament can even throw them out of office, though it has not done so in twenty-five years.

Throwing out the European Commission doesn't work in practice. The Council of Ministers, not the Commission, is responsible for final decisions. The Parliament cannot appoint a new Commission. The power of the Parliament is therefore restricted, but not insignificant. The powers of any parliament are never handed over on a silver platter. They are taken by parliament from the executive when the executive wants something from the parliament and the parliament asks something in return.

The European Parliament is unique among international organizations. There is no other international organization in which the executive body is responsible to the legislature. Further, there is no other international organization with a real parliament: not NATO, the United Nations, the Council for Mutual Economic Assistance (Comecon), or the Organization of American States. These bodies are composed of national governmental officials, politicians, and civil servants. There is no direct democratic political control of these organizations whatsoever. Nor can these institutions make decisions that are binding on all peoples of their individual members. By contrast, the Community's decisions are binding; they have the force of law in member states. They are not liable to vetoes by heads of national governments, national parliaments, or national civil servants. Therefore, the advisory and budgetary powers of the European Parliament are both consequential and unique.

How does the Parliament work? European members of Parliament are all members of their national parliaments. They are chosen by the national parliaments. Each member holds a double mandate—one national, one European. But the European Parliament is not divided on national lines; it is divided on party lines. I am a member of the socialist group in the European Parliament which currently consists of sixty-five socialists from nine countries. The chairman of our group is a German; the vice chairman is an Englishman. We do not vote as delegates from a particular country. Discipline, however, is maintained through the national parties.

The work routine of the members of Parliament is extremely rigorous and a bit gypsylike. Members of Parliament are faced with two practical problems: their own double mandates and the fact that European Community business is conducted in three different cities. Brussels is the seat of the Commission and the Council, and where we have committee meetings. Half the Parliament's plenary sessions and our secretariat are in Luxembourg. The remaining plenary sessions are held in Strasbourg. One travels all over, losing much time. The additional cost to the Community is approximately $15 million per year. It is nonsensical, but it is unlikely to change because of the pride of the national governments involved. It does present real problems because the Parliament naturally wants to be where power exists in the Community. The other problem—the dual mandate—is also bad for the Parliament.

Being a European member of Parliament and a member of a national parliament at the same time is a grueling job. One has to be in two places at the same time. How can a politician serve his national constituency and work toward reelection; and sit in Brussels, Strasbourg, and Luxembourg? When it comes to a crunch, suddenly the European parliamentarians disappear. A plane comes and they say, "Come on boys, there is a vote at home." Off they go. Why? Because when it comes to a crunch, power is where power goes. Power is in the national parliaments, and therefore, the parliamentarians leave. The double mandate is really frustrating the European Parliament very much.

What are the immediate goals of an elected parliament? The primary one is to professionalize the European Parliament. It is absolutely necessary to have a democratically elected parliament in order to make it possible for national parliaments to transfer power to European institutions. The national parliaments have already said, "We are not willing to transfer more power to the Community because the democratic control is lacking." This dilemma must be removed.

Are the direct elections being held too early? Many people have said so. They have said, "let's create power in the Community first." Well, we have been going around in the same circle for twenty-five years. DeGaulle always said, "We are against European elections because the European Parliament doesn't have powers." The Parliament replied, "Well, give us powers." And DeGaulle responded, "How can I give powers to a parliament which is not elected?" The circle is now broken. The European elections will be one of the major events in Europe, and probably in the world—nine countries putting themselves together in one democratically elected parliament to control the European Community. While the members of Parliament will be elected for five years, the Community and the Parliament will last forever. In the beginning, the Parliament will have little power, but in the long run, it will have more. A directly elected parliament is the future for Europe.

Direct Elections and the Political Party Structure
Martin Bangemann

When the national parties considered how they would participate in the elections, they faced two alternatives: to remain within the national party systems and work exclusively within their own borders, or to build European parties with common platforms, unified leadership, and internal discipline. The result of this choice underscores the reality of a unifying Europe: Almost all the parties have chosen to try to establish European-wide parties. They have worked hard to build common platforms and to develop a functioning organization.

There are three new European parties. The European Popular party is a combination of all Christian Democratic parties and the Conservative parties of the Community. The Federation of Liberal Democratic parties is a union of several Liberal parties. And the Federation of Democratic Socialists is the Socialist parties' organization. These federations are different from other organizations that existed before. For instance, the Socialist International and the Liberal International parties were simply institutions for broad discussion; they did not have the right to make binding final decisions on the members. The new European parties do have the power to bind their members to joint decisions.

An example from my own federation will illustrate the point. In order to build a political party, there must be some form of democratic structure which both permits an open debate of important issues and guarantees that once a decision has been taken, it will be supported by all the members. When we organized our party, there were two Liberal parties in Denmark that considered joining us. One of them entered our organization, and then left us. Why? We had decided democratically to favor a supernational structure for the European union and a common defense policy in the future. All of the national parties in the federation were then bound to support these policies and to campaign for them. The Danish party could not accept these policies and therefore chose to leave the federation. This problem is common to all new parties. Each national party must decide whether it will join a federation, and whether it will abide by the principles of democratic procedure. The widespread acceptance by existing national parties of these new organizations is proof of the vitality of the party system in Europe.

Too frequently, professors of politics claim that traditional parties are not responding to the important problems of the day, are bound to their traditional ideologies, and are incapable of finding new and different solutions. They are wrong. The traditional parties have responded; they have built new organizations and have met the challenge of common platforms.

What, then, are the issues that dominate efforts to build platforms for the first directly elected Parliament? All the platforms of the federations cannot be spread out here, but an outline of issues dominating them can be made. The four main issues are: defining a democratic community; strengthening the elected Parliament; explaining each party's vision of the future shape of Europe; and taking a position on economic and monetary union and the role of Europe in world politics.

On the issue of defining the democratic nature of the Community, there are several matters to be tackled. We need a constitution. This will be one of the first tasks of the new directly elected Parliament. We must have a clear statement on human and civil rights to serve as a guideline for activities of the Community internally and internationally. The Parliament as an expression of democracy in the Community must be strengthened.

The Parliament was meant in the beginning to be only an advisory body. The treaty texts make that clear. But the Parliament has been slowly developing power, especially on the right to pass the budget. As parliaments in the past fought against kings, we are now fighting against the Council of Ministers. Not even the national parliaments can control the Council. When the French minister comes home and his parliament asks, "What have you done there? Why did you agree to that foolish decision?" he says, "Well you see, there was that foolish German who is always so active at the night sessions [we do have an agricultural minister who is always drinking milk and who is active in the night sessions] and he prevented me from doing the right thing.'' Our German minister comes home and says, ''You see, there are the small Danes—they are new in the Community and we have to look out for them, and therefore I wasn't able to do all you wanted me to do.'' At the European level, the Council holds its meetings secretly and the Parliament cannot control it. It is just as in the times of the kings when prime ministers were responsible only to the kings. Many of the things that have not gone well in the Community are directly related to this problem. Democratization of the Community is the most important issue of the new Parliament.

The platforms must also speak about the future development of European society. Of course, each party will have its own scenario. They will compete for votes. Up to now, Europe has been just a subject of Sunday speeches—everyone voicing high ideals but few talking of concrete matters. Now the voters will demand concrete proposals on pressing issues—unemployment, emancipation, codetermination—and the party platforms willl have to respond.

The platforms must also take positions on the most immediately pressing issues: economic and monetary union and the role of Europe in the world. Economic and monetary union will come eventually in Europe. We must prepare for it. Each of the federations will have to take positions on how to handle such matters.

Finally, we must define the position of Europe in the world. Europe has a unique opportunity. It not only can declare, but also can demonstrate, that Europe can have great influence in the world and be a partner to the developed and developing nations. This mission for Europe cannot be designed within secret circles of experts. It will be the task of a democratic Europe. We are on our way to it.

A Critical Commentary
David Marquand

Parts of what I say don't sound as optimistic as some of the things that other speakers have said. This is not because I am not optimistic; rather, it is because we need to look more clearly at some of the problems associated with this subject.

Why should we have direct elections, and what is their significance? A democratic deficit exists at present, in the sense that decisions taken by the Council of Ministers are not properly controlled by national parliaments or the European Parliament. Therefore, the Council escapes effective democratic scrutiny and control. Another, perhaps deeper, reason for direct elections is to renew the momentum of European integration. The Community is poised in an extremely delicate situation. We have made considerable gains over the last twenty years, and now must move forward quite significantly in several areas, or run the risk of losing previous gains.

Take, for example, the question of unemployment. We now have six and one-half million unemployed people in the Community, and we expect nine million new people to enter the labor force in the next few years. Unless the Community can grasp the nettle of monetary union, which I think offers the only hope of escaping from the unemployment problem, there is a very serious danger that member states will start to erect protectionist barriers not only against the outside world, but even perhaps against each other. The central acquisitions of the Community will then be placed in jeopardy. The problems of enlargement in a way are similar. If we fail to speed up and make more efficient the institutional processes of the Community, enlargement could weaken rather than strengthen us. Then we would have to ask ourselves why the Community hasn't improved its decision-making processes. The answer was given by Sir Christopher Soames when he said, "Power isn't like money. You can't print power." If somebody is going to be given power, it has to come from somebody else. And the fact of the matter is that if power is to be given to the Community institutions, it can only come from the nation-states. If there are to be Community solutions to Community problems, the nation-states will have to surrender some of the power they presently use to make decisions.

The trouble with the institutional structure of the Community today is that the forces making for greater integration in the Community are weaker than the forces that want to hold it back. The motor of integration, to use one of the cliches of Euro-speech, is the Commission. The Commission is the sole body under the treaties that has the right to put forward proposals in the areas covered by the treaties. Thus, the Commission is an extremely important body in the decision-making process of the Community. Members of the Commission are distinguished and important people; many have had very distinguished careers in national politics. But they are not elected. They do not represent anyone. They have no constituency to throw onto the scales against the constituencies of national governments. The "kings" (in Martin Bangemann's phrase) of the Council of Ministers can say truthfully to the Parliament, "Well, we are elected by our national electorates. You, the Parliament, are not elected by anybody. Neither is the Commission."

In the modern world, power comes ultimately from democratic elections. As long as the only institution in the Community that has the legitimacy of direct popular election is the Council of Ministers, the other institutions, whose job is to encourage integration, will find it very difficult to move forward. Direct elections are important at the present time precisely because they create the possibility that an institution, whose function is to look after the interests of the Community as a whole rather than the interests of the individual member states of the Community, will be able to say with truth that *it* speaks in the name of the sovereign people of Europe and therefore that it has democratic legitimacy equal to, perhaps even superior to, that of the national governments. This could fundamentally change the balance of power in the institutions of the Community.

Commentaries

Soames: One shouldn't overestimate the power of the European Parliament. I spent some years as a minister, having to justify my actions to a national parliament. I also spent some years as a commissioner, having to justify my actions to the European Parliament. I can assure you that I was much more frightened of the national parliament than I was of the European Parliament. This is the fault of the European Parliament. It is a built-in fault at the moment because it is indirectly elected and because it meets very seldom.

Once directly elected, they must meet in one place, they must be a constant feature of Community life as opposed to an occasional feature, and they must put the Commission under much more scrutiny than they have hitherto. Certainly, the Council of Ministers must be summoned to its footstool much more often. It must make the ministers frightened. No parliament has ever gotten power without grabbing it. It is never going to get it by holding out its hand and asking for it. The Parliament is going to have to say, "this is what we are going to do and this is how."

We in Europe tend to choose our executive out of our legislatures, unlike the United States. In Europe, the only way that one can become a minister, generally speaking, is through parliament. Why not choose the Commission from the European Parliament? So at least members of Parliament can be attracted by the fact that once they get there and do well, they can be nominated as commissioners and have a real job to do.

Let's not kid ourselves. A directly elected parliament will not make all the difference. What's going to make the difference is how the members handle themselves once they are in office, and the way they throw their weight around. A Commission drawn from the Parliament would itself be an elected body then, the same as the government in our own country.

Patijn: When one hears Sir Christopher, one has the idea that he has been four years in the European Commission with 198 parliamentarians sitting like cats purring on his lap, which is, of course, nonsense. What is the actual situation? You ask a nonpowerful Parliament to control a nonpowerful European Commission. The Parliament can be blamed for not controlling the Commission effectively enough. Buy why should we sweep away the

European Commission, when in nine out of ten cases, it is on the Parliament's side against the Council of Ministers? Why should the Parliament be rough with the only club in Brussels that has some influence in the closed sessions of the Council of Ministers? We could grill the Commission for more information and initiatives, of course, but the group that really needs grilling is the Council of Ministers. The real problem is that the decision-making process is not balanced among the government, the Commission, and the Parliament—the normal situation—but is centered on an all-powerful senate joined by a weak executive that can only make proposals, and a weak legislature that can only give advice. This is an idiotic situation.

Two things could be done: make the Commission the secretariat of the Council so that the Commission loses its independence and the Parliament confronts the Council directly; or remove the Council and make the Commission the government responsible to the Parliament. Both solutions have great advantages, but the reality of the situation is different from that implied by Sir Christopher. The Parliament has tried for twenty-five years to increase its powers and to improve the democratic process of the Community. It has proposed that it have the final say in the nomination of commissioners, that the Council of Ministers have open sessions, and that the Parliament have greater legislative power. These proposals have always had the support of the Commission and have always been refused by the Council. The national governments do not want the Community to have so much power! Far from doing nothing in the last twenty-five years, Parliament has been the busiest body in the Community. Yet we have come only 5 percent of the way toward a normal democratic legislative process. If we are to go forward, the Parliament and the Commission must work together.

Marquand: I am speaking as somebody who works for the Commission. I am constantly surprised by how unaggressive European parliamentarians are toward us. They could be a lot more aggressive than they are. I am not going to tell them how; they have to work that out for themselves. Mention has been made of the budgetary powers of the Parliament. In fact, I would have thought that by using the budgetary powers of Parliament, it would be possible to force changes of policy to a much greater extent than is achieved at the present time. The reason is very simple: the members of the European Parliament are not primarily European politicians elected under a European mandate. Once European politicians are elected, they will have to go back to their constituents and justify themselves. People will ask them hard questions. I do not think that the first elected Parliament will seize new powers; that's really for the Parliament after next—but the first one ought to make full and aggressive use of the powers they in fact already possess.

We ought to be cautious in the short term, because we have had too many experiences in the Community with grandiose slogans and high hopes that failed to be realized immediately. The result has been disillusionment, perhaps even despair. Yet there are immediate problems to be faced. The Commission has put forward plans to relaunch the idea of monetary union, for example. I believe this to be absolutely essential. But who is going to run the monetary union? What sort of institution will decide the level of money supply in Europe, presumably a responsibility that would be transferred to the European level? What will be the relationship between that body and the European Parliament? It seems to me unthinkable that one could transfer powers of that importance to a body sitting in a kind of platonic void deciding, out of a sense of inherent superiority, what should be done to the levels of unemployment throughout Europe. An elected body must be made responsible somehow or other. It seems to me very important to decide on the role of the European Parliament in that regard.

Bangemann: The fight between the national parliaments and the European Parliament will be a very fierce one, fiercer than the fight between the European Parliament and the Council of Ministers. Although it is true that a minister ultimately represents voters, he really represents a government. It will be an easy task for the elected European Parliament to fight the ministers with the argument that they represent the people while the ministers represent the government. But how will the European Parliament fight the national parliaments? They, too, represent the voters directly. They, too, are democratic bodies. It will be some time before areas of competence will be sorted out between the European Parliament and the national parliaments. Until then, a bridge must be built betwen the two bodies. A certain number of dual mandates would be useful. They could prevent the national parliaments from becoming egoistic.

Marquand: What will be the relationship between the European Parliament and national parliaments? Is there a danger that perhaps the European Parliament will be a sort of stratospheric body sitting grandly in Strasbourg and in Luxembourg, but in fact will not be noticed by the real political forces in the member states? If we are to avoid that, what kind of institutions are going to have to be created so as to ensure proper coordination between national and Community levels? What is going to be the role of the parties? This question is one of the most crucial. An election in any democratic country is about a choice between different conceptions of society and different policies. But the European political parties that are being formed make up within themselves an enormously wide variety of ideological positions. Are the programs that the parties intend to present likely to be meaningful programs? Are they, in fact, going to present real choices? Or, are they simply going to be collections of euphoric pieties about the sanctity of motherhood and the virtues of democracy? It is very easy to draw up a platform that means nothing. It is not so easy to draw up a platform that presents a real choice.

Patijn: A major goal of the directly elected Parliament is to make it possible for the national parliaments to transfer power to European institutions. The national parliaments have made it clear many times: "We are not willing to transfer more power to the Community without democratic control." This dilemma must be solved by establishing democratic control at the European level, that is, the Parliament. Such action will also guarantee democracy in the participating countries.

With elections to the European Parliament occurring every five years, every member country promises to have a functioning democracy. If they do not fulfill the letter of the law, by sending colonels, sergeants, or corporals, they will not be accepted in the Parliament. They will be thrown out of the Parliament and the Community as well. Direct elections reinforce democracy throughout Europe.

Marquand: The issues that could divide the European Parliament are not the same ones that divide national parliaments. The issues that need to be settled at the European level—energy policy, industrial policy, monetary union—do not resemble the ideological stands of the national parties. In the Commission, for example, the socialist commissioners do not vote together against the nonsocialists on these issues. The European issues that have to be settled don't necessarily fit into the ideological boxes along which national parties are constructed. If I think about it over a longish time scale, I can imagine a party structure emerging at the European level to settle European issues that would be rather different from a national party structure that must try to settle national issues. This probably is heresy to the two active members of the European Parliament who are here, but that's the way I see it.

At the moment, we have the problem of the double mandate. The fact is that individual members of the European Parliament are really elected to do a job at the national level, and they take on their shoulders the burden of membership in the European Parliament as an act of idealism. They are not, in fact, elected to do that job. It is an impossible situation. On the other hand, they do have strength because they are members of a national parliament. If Dr. Bangemann doesn't like what the Council of Ministers does, he can at least go back to the Bundestag and give hell to the German minister who is representing Germany in the Council.

Patijn: A different European party structure from national structures is of course a possibility, as David Marquand describes it. But I do not think it likely. In my country of Holland, the north area is relatively poor and suffers from 8 to 9 percent unemployment. In the European Parliament, where the regional funds are meant to balance growth of the various areas within Europe, the north of Holland seems eligible for help from the regional funds. But next to me sits a Labor parliamentarian from western Ireland, which for twenty-five years has had 25 percent unemployment and massive emigration. Indeed, there are more people from his constituency living in New York City than in the region itself. Then I shut my mouth, forget my national pride and national priorities, and give the money to Ireland instead. That is the problem one faces in the European Parliament. We call it socialistic solidarity. In this case, solidarity means that you do something for somebody else that you wanted to do for yourself. These problems arise, but you can explain them at home, even in northern Holland. National solutions give way to European solutions because they are more important. It is certainly right to give the money to Ireland.

It is impossible to be in both places at the same time. All the stories that say the European Parliament can only be run if Tindemans, Brandt, Schmidt, Callaghan, and Heath sit in it, mean that these people either would give up their jobs at home or make fools of the voters by taking up seats in the European Parliament and not fulfilling their jobs. This is nonsense. We have to form our own leaders.

Who will be in this European Parliament? It is very clear from the amount of work concerned that if you belong to a political elite at home and want to remain there, you are not going to run for the European Parliament. If you run for the Parliament and want to become part of the political elite at the European level, forget about being in the political elite at home. One cannot do both things at the same time. The European Parliament will have its own political elite in the long run.

Schaetzel: One of the things that bothers me about direct elections is how to attract highly qualified people to run for a Parliament that has no power and is not likely to have power in the natural sense. If they are elected, will they wish to stay in the Parliament if they don't see the ability to do something? And how can they respond to an irate constituent with the rationalization, "Well, I can't do anything because I don't have any power"?

Patijn: Will they remain? Yes, I would forecast that about 75 percent of the elected members will have only the European mandate. They will be professional European parliamentarians, doing a job, getting a salary. Unless they want to quit politics, they will try to remain. As for the problem of constituency, I wonder if Ambassador Schaetzel's hypothetical question is accurate. If a man belongs to the French National Assembly in the Fifth Republic, can he really explain to his constituency what he is doing in Paris? Most of the powers of the Assembly have been stripped. The budgetary powers of the European Parliament are more powerful than those of the French Assembly. I am not going to say that for every constituency in Europe we have things to explain; but there is much to be explained: regional, social, and industrial policies. The elections are about real issues, not Sunday speeches on whether one wants a federal or confederal Europe. The parliamentarians will have much to take back to their voters.

Marquand: What is going to happen after direct elections? Will European Parliamentarians be able to take European rather than national positions? This is terribly important. At the moment, members of the European Parliament don't have to justify policies to their constituents in the way that a national member of parliament must. Because the European Community is not currently very sexy, people know little about what happens there. There is a real danger that when members of Parliament are directly elected and must justify their votes, it will be more difficult to take a trans-European stand that happens to hurt the interests of particular constituents.

Bangemann: During the time I have been a member of the European Parliament, it has divided on national lines only twice. Of course, the Council of Ministers is broken down on national lines. Normally in the Parliament, the lines of division for political decisions are political alliances, not national alliances. There are occasions when national lines predominate, such as in the fishery issue, when representatives from Britain and Ireland stood against the rest of the Parliament. It may happen again that national lines affect decisions of the Community, but the institution most likely to overcome this is a directly elected parliament. Therefore, direct elections are crucial to strengthening the Community.

The European Community is best known for its failures rather than its successes. The Community must heighten awareness of its successes. A simple example occurred to one of my liberal colleagues in the German parliament. A piece of legislation that he favored was stopped in the parliament by the German government. Six months later, he discovered that the initiative to stop it had come from Brussels. "How had it happened?" he asked. The German government had gotten the European government to take the necessary steps. That was the moment of his European enlightenment. He realized that there was a European reality.

The man in the street understands this reality too, perhaps better than the politician in his narrow borders. That's my hope for the elections and for Europe.

Note

1. Jean Monnet, *Memoirs,* trans. Richard Mayne (New York: Doubleday & Co, 1978), pp. 521, 523.

5 Coordinating Economic Policies

A Choice of Strategies

Tension between the forces of economic interdependence and those of national political autonomy has caused governments, as we noted in chapter 1, to devise specific strategies for reconciling conflicts between economic and political objectives. Some governments, we observed, have turned protectionist, retreating from the process of internationalization into a more self-sufficient world, but one whose economic rewards are not as generous as the benefits of specialization and trade. Other governments, usually in concert with many nations, have tried to alter international monetary and trading systems in ways that delegate the awkward processes of adjusting to disequilibriums to the marketplace so that they may be freer to use the tools of government policy to achieve domestic social and political objectives. And still others have tried to institute strategies that involve them in systematic international efforts at cooperation and coordination of economic policies; efforts, as it were, that reconcile domestic political arrangements to the forces of economic internationalization. The focus of this chapter will be on, though by no means exclusively, the latter of these three strategies.

Earlier in the postwar period, efforts at international cooperation and coordination were focused primarily on what has been called "negative" coordination, which means a set of rules designed to discourage the manipulation of trading relations or exchange rates for the purpose of alleviating domestic economic or social problems. Negative coordination is continuing, of course, in the quest for workable limits on the freedom of nations to "manage" floating exchange rates, as described below.

But with the rise of concern recently about poor macroeconomic performance in the world economy, there has developed a feeling that positive coordination also is required. Such coordination can take many different forms. The simplest may only involve an exchange of information among cooperating nations about their intended macroeconomic policies in the immediate future. Given this information, each then may work out more fully for itself policies that are consistent with the policies of others. The process obviously is iterative, requiring more than one consultation if subsequent adjustments to policies are significant. The need for this simple type of coordination is evident in the recent history of policy responses to common business cycle signals: By and large, nations have tended to overrespond to the signals of peaks and troughs in recent cycles of world business activity, by failing to adequately anticipate similar actions by other large nations. As a result, needless degrees of restraint or stimulus were begun, worsening overall economic performance for all nations. Common sense suggests that this type of consultation is desirable and overdue.

More ambitious forms of cooperation may involve attempts by certain nations to coordinate the setting of broad macroeconomic objectives and the selection of policies to achieve them. Both types of coordination have been attempted recently. Stimulated especially by research and discussions held under the aegis of the Organization for Economic Cooperation and Development, the principal western powers have been challenged to coordinate their objectives as if they were locomotives pulling a train (the 1976-77 version) and as if they were key ships in a convoy (the 1977-78 version), on the reasonable premise that compatible policy targets in the largest and richest nations will, if properly implemented, help all other nations (cabooses, freighters) reach their destinations more easily. We shall explore below a few of the intriguing difficulties of moving in trains or convoys.

If compatible sets of policy targets can be agreed upon by participating nations, the task of achieving them simultaneously may also require considerable cooperation and coordination. The problems are both theoretical and procedural. In the first place, nations willing to negotiate international agreements concerning the uses of particular policies under certain circumstances need to have similar understandings about how the pieces of a national and a world economy fit together, and especially how changes in key economic variables influence each other and ultimately shape the performance of national economies. This kind of theoretical understanding is weaker today than at any time in the last four decades, unfortunately, leaving policy-makers with much too broad a choice among alternative models of the economic system to assure similarity of views across nations. The comments of Robert Solomon later in this chapter, notwithstanding, economists are no longer precisely sure how to treat an aggregate economy suffering simultaneously from, say, high rates of unemployment, excessive inflation, large government deficits, and seemingly chronic deficits or surpluses in the balance of payments. Procedurally, the problem is one of reaching agreement, even after the development of common theoretical understanding, about the particular policy tools that should be coordinated. Institutional differences among nations, including differences in the traditional roles particular policies have been assigned in certain countries, make the negotiation of international agreements about such things as the level and structure of interest rates, monetary growth rates, exchange rates, and the uses of international reserves extremely tedious and difficult.

This background of caution about the pitfalls of coordinating economic policies helps to put in perspective the history of progress toward economic integration within the European Community. As described by Ambassador Spaak in chapter 3 and by Sir Christopher Soames in chapter 2, development during the last twenty years of multiple common institutions among the six original member nations of the European Community, now expanded to nine, can be counted as a truly remarkable achievement, despite the vexing and very human shortcomings of present arrangements which they and the parliamentarians of chapter 4 so candidly confess. Thus, the initiative launched in 1978 to establish no less than a new European monetary system as quickly as possible takes on added meaning as an ambitious plan for the accommodation of traditional domestic political autonomy to the needs of international economic integration. Professor Forte outlines later in this chapter some special difficulties of rationalizing Community monetary policies.

Like the Schuman Plan of 1950 which led to the pooling of Europe's coal and steel industries under a supranational authority, and ultimately to the formation and consolidation of the European Community itself, the proposal of a new European monetary system highlights the enormous diplomatic costs that must be incurred in order to implement an international system of cooperation and coordination. In a world requiring vast outlays of scarce technical and diplomatic resources to negotiate and manage viable structures of trade, investment, aid, development, payments, and exploitation of the global commons, timid individuals and nations may be forgiven for wondering whether a strategy of international cooperation and coordination is really appropriate, particularly in cases when the alternatives of protectionism or economic accommodation seem to be genuinely available strategies. Indeed, it is for this very reason that governments in practice are likely to try most available strategies simultaneously. As the comments of conference participants illustrate, nations groping for new ways to reconcile tensions between the internationalization of economic systems and the nationalization of political systems no doubt will end up with an eclectic strategy bearing fleeting resemblance to all three kinds of strategies described above.

The two shocks to the international system that best account for recent efforts at macroeconomic coordination were the collapse of the Bretton Woods system in 1971-73, and the stubborn persistence of what has come to be called stagflation—the coexistence of substantial unemployment and rising prices—in most national economies since the bottom of the 1974-75 world recession. These two experiences have combined with general perceptions of increased policy interdependence to focus special attention, even at the highest policy levels, on the need for new institutional means of coordinating the performances of leading national economies. Indeed, the beginning recently of regular summit meetings on economic affairs has dramatized for the public the sense of urgency now felt among world leaders to develop new concepts of collective economic leadership.

Reforming the Monetary System

Of all the institutional arrangements entered into by cooperating nations after World War II, the international monetary system designed at Bretton Woods came closest to being a genuinely formal system. Anchored in the Articles of Agreement of the International Monetary Fund, the system consisted of four closely related elements, each in its way meant to correct a shortcoming of previous systems: It established an "adjustable peg" regime of exchange rates which obligated each member nation to declare a par value for its currency and to intervene in the exchange markets to keep it near the peg, except when, after full consultation, it was permitted to change the par value in order to acknowledge fundamentally new circumstances; it established the IMF system of subscriptions and quotas in order to provide nations with a supplementary source of foreign currencies to engage in exchange stabilization activities; it established a code of conduct for member nations which generally forbade them from engaging in discriminatory currency practices or exchange-control regulations; and it formally obligated member nations to consult and cooperate on monetary matters, principally through institutional channels provided at the International Monetary Fund.

Though multilateral in formal design, in actual practice the Bretton Woods system was highly centralized from the start. After the war, only the United States and a few smaller American nations were able to pledge full cooperation with the Articles of Agreement; most other nations were so devastated by the war that they simply could not forswear discriminatory practices and make their currencies immediately convertible. In the breach, the United States agreed in effect to take over as money manager of the world, at least until the conditions for a smoothly functioning international economy as envisioned at Bretton Woods could be achieved. Its duties in this assignment consisted of maintaining a relatively open market for the exports of other nations; assuring a generous flow of long-term loans and grants to the rest of the world, first by offering Marshall Plan assistance and other forms of aid, and later by encouraging expansion of the New York capital market; and eventually establishing a relatively liberal lending policy for making short-term loans to governments suffering from balance of payments crises.

In short, by taking on this role of world monetary manager the United States agreed to subordinate some of its short-term economic interests to a longer-term objective of strengthening the economies of other free-world nations. The advantages to America were nonetheless significant. Fighting the Cold War cost money, and America's new position gave it the privilege of spending as freely as it thought necessary to promote the national interest. If it thought that more needed to be spent on the economic recovery of potential allies in Europe and Japan and on its sizeable security forces overseas than seemed possible under ordinary balance of payments constraints, it simply ran deficits in its own balance of payments, thus vesting the dollar with a special privilege not available to other currencies. Foreign holders of dollars conceded policy autonomy to the Americans, because the purposes to which American policies were directed presumably benefited them; in effect, they granted America the right to print international IOUs in return for America's willingness to shoulder responsibility for the economic stability and military security of the noncommunist world.

But the bargain began to come unglued in the 1960s, when the size of American deficits grew alarmingly and the nations of Europe and Japan no longer felt as dependent, politically and strategically, on the goodwill of the United States. By then, the system had developed several apparent weaknesses. Although the system foresaw the use of exchange rate changes to adjust fundamental payment imbalances, they were not used extensively because they were fraught with both political and economic risks. As the numeraire currency of the system, moreover, the dollar was locked into its par value even more inextricably than the currencies of other countries. This meant that adjustment took the form much too often of adjustments in domestic economic policies, actions that were clearly alien to the spirit of Bretton Woods. It meant also that American business and financial interests became increasingly agitated as progressive overvaluation of the dollar undermined their competitive positions in home and world markets.

Another of the system's weaknesses was its provision of international liquidity. So long as the principal source of additions to central bank reserves was dollar IOUs generated by deficits in the American balance of payments, confidence in the longer-term convertibility of reserve holdings was undermined. This became an especially critical issue when, as the American commitment in Viet Nam mounted, the size of American deficits suddenly outpaced the growth in the need for additional reserves in other nations. And still another weakness—perhaps the most fundamental of all, in political terms—was the inherent asymmetry of a system that accorded one nation so much more power than others in the determination of broad economic and strategic policies. Economic and political changes wrought in the world since the 1950s had made the hegemony of the dollar an anachronism politically, calling for considerably more symmetry in the design of future monetary systems.

To be sure, governments tried cooperatively during the latter part of the 1960s to correct these deficiencies, partly with greater exchange rate variation, partly with the introduction of a new source of reserves called Special Drawing Rights (SDR), and partly with more intense consultation and mutual lending assistance during times of monetary crises. But the leaks of confidence from the system could not be stemmed, leading in August, 1971, to the inevitable inconvertibility of dollars into gold, and in March, 1973, to abandonment of any attempt to maintain fixed exchange rates.

Ever since then, the governments of the world have been trying to create a new international monetary system, one with more capacity than the old to promote smooth adjustments to disturbances in the world economy, to assure adequacy and control over the availability of international reserves, to enhance the capacities of individual nations to carry out their own macroeconomic plans and objectives, and to reduce the operational asymmetry of the system. Plagued by the outbreak of hyperinflation and then a serious world recession, its planners have repeatedly had to settle for less than full reform. The results of their deliberations over a four-year period are now embodied in amendments to the IMF Articles of Agreement which are in the process of being ratified by member nations.

These amendments permit "freedom of choice" among exchange rate regimes, ratifying the system of "managed floating" which has in fact emerged since 1973. Thus, while the dollar and several other major currencies may float more or less freely, some European countries may continue to attempt to maintain a joint float—the so-called snake—or move gradually toward a common European Currency Unit (ECU), and still others, notably most developing countries, may peg their currencies to one or a "basket" of major currencies as they see fit. The IMF continues to have primary oversight of the international monetary system, including the obligation under these amendments to "exercise firm surveillance over the exchange rate policies of members" and to "adopt specific principles for the guidance of all members with respect to those policies." The amendments also reaffirmed the objective of making SDRs "the principal reserve asset in the international monetary system," and authorized the modest implementing step of reducing the roles of gold in the system. In related actions, member nations of the IMF authorized general increases in quotas in order to enlarge the capacity of the IMF to help members finance short-term reversible balance of payments fluctuations.

How much do these reforms assist the nations of the world in re-creating a salubrious climate for beneficial international economic intercourse? Do they, in particular, reinforce the inclination of national governments to adopt one or another of the strategies outlined above to deal with the tensions between international economic integration and national political autonomy?

The decision to allow greater flexibility in exchange rate regimes, though largely forced on member nations by the course of events, nonetheless has had the effect of building greater automaticity into the adjustment process. This development allowed the dollar in particular to be adjusted downward in value, enhancing the competitiveness of American goods and relieving the pressures domestic groups put on government to turn strongly protectionist. Ironically, the renewed slide of dollar values during 1978 strengthened protectionist sentiment felt by those abroad who are fearful that even lower dollar values will weaken the market for foreign goods. Flexibility of exchange rates also has enabled governments to decide for themselves how many international reserves to accumulate. Countries today can choose the rate of accumulation they prefer by managing the foreign exchange rate, thus greatly reducing the need of the system to provide supranational control of the volume of international liquidity. It seems likely, therefore, that greater automaticity in the design of the new international monetary system has, in general, discouraged adoption of the protectionist strategy and encouraged attempts to insulate domestic political decisions from external market forces in other than protectionist ways.

It should be noted, even so, that a system of managed floating does not afford the degree of domestic policy insulation that is posited in the theories of freely fluctuating exchange rates. In a world of managed interventions in exchange markets and free mobility of money capital across international boundaries, strong threads of interdependence persist, linking disturbances originating elsewhere to rates of unemployment, inflation, and growth at home. Flexibility has probably reduced the international transmission of disturbances, but it certainly has not eliminated it.

Nor has reform of the international monetary system much influenced many qualities of the dollar that made it special in the Bretton Woods period. The dollar continues to serve, for example, as the principal intervention currency and as the premier transactions currency for private purposes. It does so in part because there is no completely adequate substitute for it at the present time, and more fundamentally because the economic size of the United States, the strength of its capital markets, and its freedom from exchange controls make the dollar a very efficient medium of exchange. The United States seems, moreover, still to be ready to play a more passive role in managing its balance of payments; this attitude makes it easier for countries with strong preferences for balance of payments surpluses to achieve them, especially in the presence of large surpluses among the OPEC countries. Thus, considerable asymmetry remains in today's international monetary system.

It is not very clear when we may expect a significant rival to the dollar's key currency roles to emerge. The recent reform discussions held out the hope that Special Drawing Rights may eventually become the primary reserve asset held by central banks. Yet they now constitute only 5 percent of international reserves, and their yield, reconstitution commitments, and newness stand in their way of rapid substitution for dollars. Renewed interest by Europeans in a European monetary system, stimulated in part by the disorderly fall of the dollar in exchange markets during 1978, may also produce a potentially attractive unit of account which someday could supplement the transactions and intervention roles of the dollar. But these innovations will take time to develop and diffuse, granting the dollar a significant plurality in use for the foreseeable future.

Coordinating Stabilization Policies

Having reformed the international monetary system—more or less—after collapse of the Bretton Woods system earlier in the decade, policy-makers now have turned their collective attention to ways of reversing the trend toward poor macroeconomic performance which has plagued the Western world since about 1973. How is it possible, they are asking, to boost rates of employment and growth cooperatively without running the risks of greater inflation, protectionism, and excessive fluctuations in exchange rates?

The question does not yield easy answers. In the first place, stagflation is a puzzling phenomenon for economic theorists. As economic slack in the economy grows and unemployment rises, inflation is supposed to abate, according to modern Phillips Curve analysis. The reverse also should be true: a country ought to be able to achieve higher rates of output and employment if it is willing to tolerate a higher rate of price increase. But the experience with stagflation in recent years has now produced an alternative theory, a theory which suggests that inflation, except possibly in the very short run, makes the attainment of higher rates of employment and growth less rather than more likely. The idea behind the latter theory is that people suffering from inflation sooner or later come to expect it in the future, and that they adjust their wage demands and consumption patterns accordingly. Thus, attempts to reduce the unemployment rate below its "natural" level are self-defeating.

This theoretical quandary is complicated further by not knowing precisely at what level of unemployment and excess capacity prices start to rise in a Phillips Curve world or, alternatively, how much unemployment is "natural" in a monetarist's world. There is reason to believe that increases since 1973 in the price of energy have permanently reduced the level of potential output in all industrial countries; estimates for the United States indicate, for example, that potential output is now more than 4 percent below the trend existing before the oil price increase. This fact may indicate that the amount of slack in western economies, as traditionally measured, may exaggerate the degree of stimulus they may absorb before beginning to experience unwanted inflation. Even so, it is clear from the remarks of

Messrs. Forte, Hara, and Solomon in this chapter—all of who are distinguished economists—that in their view anyway, there is sufficient slack in most western economies to warrant monetary and fiscal stimulus without great fear of additional inflation.

Professor Forte neatly introduces another source of controversy about the treatment of slack economies: How is the stimulus to be applied, once agreement has been reached on the desirable degree of stimulus in the aggregate? Rightly or wrongly, most nations have gotten the impression that expansion in their export sectors is less inflationary than an equivalent increase in aggregate demand arising from stimuli applied to domestic sectors. As a consequence, strong and weak nations alike prefer export-led expansion to the home-grown variety. Yet, as Professor Forte points out, not every nation can expect to fuel its expansion with rapid expansion of exports, and especially not the locomotive economies that must sell their exports to partner countries whose financial viability and balance of payments situations cannot sustain major increases of imports. Nonetheless, political pressures from domestic exporters with underutilized capacity are mounting rapidly in Europe and Japan—and some would admit in America, too—to force even the locomotive governments to adopt export-led expansionary policies. Under these circumstances, controversy is inevitable.

The problem of cooperatively boosting employment and growth is also a problem of reconciling different national preferences. Not all nations fear unemployment as much as the British do, or inflation as much as the Germans do. Although these are grossly oversimplified caricatures of complex national attitudes—attitudes which, by the way, are changing rapidly for a variety of reasons—they nevertheless help to identify still another source of controversy among nations in the quest for coordinated economic stabilization.

Organizationally, as Professor Gerald Meier points out in this chapter, the leading industrial countries have concentrated their search for feasible ways to coordinate stabilization policies in the forums of the International Monetary Fund. Under its amended Articles of Agreement, the IMF is directed to assume a central and active role in the surveillance of member countries' exchange rate policies and other policies that have a bearing on exchange rates. Thus, in the formal documentation at least, the IMF is to be concerned as much about countries' monetary policies, the mix of fiscal and monetary policies, incomes policies, and trade policies (for the simple reason that these "other" policies have a direct effect on exchange rates in a floating rate system), as it is to watch their direct interventions in exchange markets and their uses of controls over capital flows or other international transactions.

Needless to say, these are delicate matters over which national policymakers in the breach will give up their traditional controls only with the greatest reluctance. Accordingly, work has been going on for several years at the IMF to develop politically feasible international guidelines of acceptable conduct in the management of exchange rates. Alternative criteria for judging appropriate conduct have been proposed—including indicators of reserve movements, target zones of acceptable exchange rate variation, reference rates, indicators of aggressiveness—and they all have been found wanting, ostensibly on the grounds that desirable balance of payments and exchange rate behavior is too complex to be adequately captured by a set of exchange rate or reserve indicators. As a result, the IMF now seems to have decided that acceptable norms must be built up over time from the experience of dealing case by case with concrete situations. This judgmental approach probably is the best that can be expected in the absence of agreement among national governments on a more highly structured approach to international surveillance.

In the meantime, as we noted earlier, the members of the European Community pushed ahead with plans for a "common approach" to the economic problems facing the Community, including "closer monetary cooperation" which it hoped would lead to establishment of a genuinely new European monetary system. In words reminiscent of calls for locomotives and convoys, the "common approach" agreed to by the Council of Ministers included the direction that "countries without inflation and balance of payments problems [should] do more to increase domestic demand, in particular investment demand and [the] rate of economic growth [while] countries with steeply rising prices will first concentrate in particular on undesirably inflationary developments." The Council also made clear in its public announcements that closer monetary cooperation among member states would require measures "to strengthen the economies of the less prosperous member countries," a condition for its success spelled out clearly by Professor Forte in this chapter.

In the event, a new European Monetary System (EMS) was finally put into effect in April, 1979, after four frustrating months during which France demanded changes in the Community's Common Agricultural Policy as a condition for her ratification of the EMS arrangements. The new system reaffirms fixed exchange rates among member currencies, even as their "zone of monetary stability" floats against outside currencies (much like the "snake" it replaces has floated); supports the parities with a large credit fund denominated in European currency units; and provides for exchange market interventions in member currencies rather than dollars in order to avoid harmful side effects on the dollar. Important, too, is the implication that members will coordinate policies sufficiently to narrow existing disparities in growth and inflation rates, and that they will strive for a lower average rate of inflation than recently experienced.

The degree of policy coordination implied by these ambitious European schemes is very high indeed, marking the European initiatives as genuine tests of the limits to which sovereign nations in today's world will subordinate domestic political control to international economic interests. There is a feeling shared by many observers of international economic affairs that knowledge is much too imperfect and forecasts are much too undependable for these conceptual and organizational sources of controversey to be easily resolved. This uncertainty means that the particular biases of nations about the origins and treatment of macroeconomic events tend to be brought to the bargaining table and to be translated there into perceived conflicts of interest. It means also that the risks of changing present practices loom larger, despite the evident sacrifices in potential output and employment that existing macroeconomic policies seem to have willed particular nations. While the initiatives in Europe toward more common approaches deserve careful attention and encouragement, these seasoned observers are understandably skeptical that policy harmonization and monetary union can be achieved even by Europeans in the foreseeable future.

Instead of achieving finely specified guidelines for national conduct in the exchange markets or carefully fashioned treaties of monetary union, the world is much more likely to make progress coordinating stabilization policies in the less formal and pluralistic atmosphere of meetings of central bank heads and finance ministers, and of "summit" discussions among the political leaders of the leading industrial countries. Summitry, in particular, seems an appropriate format for working out the broad outlines of cooperative behavior because its national participants are identical to those charged with primary responsibility within currency blocs for managing floating exchange rates. Indeed, the dominance of a few large industrial nations in the process of developing workable concepts of macroeconomic coordination may now be even greater than ever, despite the rapid spread of development in some other parts of the world and the cries from every quarter for a new international economic order.

Microeconomic Coordination

The distinction between macroeconomic and microeconomic coordination is not especially sharp.[1] Variations in the indices of aggregative economic activity and in the macroeconomic policies that affect them inevitably are felt unevenly by particular regions, sectors, and groups of the economy—which is to say, the microeconomic actors of the economy. In a similar vein, improved performance in the microeconomic parts of the economy greatly enhances the potential for growth and stability in the whole economy. Indeed, the treatment of stagflation to which virtually every economist subscribes in the long run is the reduction or elimination of of anticompetitive restrictions in many labor, capital, and product markets—restrictions that prevent these markets from carrying out the adjustments that would greatly alleviate inflationary and recessionary tendencies. In short, efforts to improve the management of macroeconomic problems and progress toward the creation of better ways to treat microeconomic problems are complementary, each reinforcing the other in quest of better economic performance.

Whereas attempts to coordinate macroeconomic policies are rather recent phenomena in international diplomacy, measures to assure better microeconomic performance in the international economy have been a principal objective of diplomatic discussions for many decades. The postwar international trading system, for example, is the product of negotiations commenced at Bretton Woods and continued under the aegis of the General Agreement on Tariffs and Trade. The most recent round of multilateral negotiations carried on under the GATT is the so-called Tokyo Round, which now is approaching completion after more than four years of almost continuous conversations among delegates of GATT member nations. Its history, told with a backdrop of the guiding principles of the GATT, illustrates rather well the difficulties and frustrations of reaching agreement on a common framework for microeconomic coordination.

The GATT is anchored in four guiding principles of trade liberalization:[2] that trade concessions negotiated between two or more countries will be promptly extended to all member countries—the so-called most-favored-nation or nondiscrimination principle; that tariffs and other explicit barriers to international trade will be reduced as a means of encouraging trade expansion; that trade concessions given by one country will be matched by equivalent concessions granted by the other negotiating party or parties—the so-called reciprocity principle; and that the GATT will seek a world trading order or set of "ground rules" that limits the application of commercial policies other than tariffs and provides for their multilateral surveillance. All four principles are under attack in the Tokyo Round.

The nondiscrimination principle was challenged long before the advent of the Tokyo Round by the proliferation of preferential trading arrangements among groups of neighboring or politically allied nations. Ironically, it was the United States, the primary champion of the global approach to trade liberalization in the postwar period, that in the GATT endorsed exemption of full customs unions and free trade areas from the obligations of most-favored-nation treatment and that urged the major industrial powers of Europe into forming the European Economic Community. But several less comprehensive preferential arrangements have been developed more recently, including the Lomé Convention of 1975 between the European Community and a growing number of African, Asian, and

Caribbean countries; it is described in greater detail in the next chapter. Because of the selective nature of these arrangements, their "trade-diverting" effects which restrict and distort international trade are likely to outweigh their "trade-creating" effects which enhance efficiency and the growth of multilateral trade, contrary to the balance struck between these effects in most comprehensive arrangements.

The nondiscrimination principle has been challenged also by the proliferation of tariff and nontariff barriers against the importation of particular products from particular countries. Since the present GATT "escape clause" (permitting temporary trade restrictions when trade patterns change abruptly and important domestic interests are threatened) is regarded by most member nations as too restrictive, many members, including the United States, have developed their own safeguard mechanisms that violate GATT requirements. Notable among the safeguards are "voluntary export restraints" negotiated at either the governmental or industry level. These restraints, such as those forced on the Japanese when American textiles, television, bicycle, and steel producers felt threatened by imports, are simply disguised forms of quotas that severely restrict trade and force what trade is left into narrowly discriminatory channels. Professor Meier explores the problem further in this chapter.

Both kinds of lapses from the nondiscrimination principle repeatedly undermined progress in the Tokyo Round. Rather than continue frontal assaults on preferential arrangements and the uses of safeguard mechanisms, which seemed futile, the negotiators finally agreed on a series of "codes" governing technical barriers to trade, government procurement procedures, import licensing procedures, customs valuation, and subsidies, which it is hoped will salvage some vestige of the nondiscrimination principle by making more transparent, and therefore more subject to multilateral surveillance, some of the practices that have most undermined GATT most-favored-nation obligations. Significantly, the tentative agreement which finally was reached in April, 1979, still did not include agreement on a code covering safeguards against injurious imports, the working out of which was "under intensive negotiation" according to GATT press releases.

The second GATT principle, trade liberalization through the reduction of barriers, has been realized to a very considerable degree. Successive rounds of tariff reductions have lowered nominal rates to modest levels and have made some progress toward limiting nontariff restrictions. When implemented over the next eight years, for example, agreements reached in the Tokyo Round will lead to a one-third reduction in U.S. industrial tariffs, a one-quarter cut in Japanese tariffs, and about a one-fifth reduction in Community tariffs. By the same token, these rounds—and especially the Tokyo Round—have revealed how very hard it is to lower tariffs and quantitative restrictions whose removal are likely to create painful and disruptive political and social effects at home. There are definite limits, therefore, to the ability of GATT to eliminate still more distortions of international trade by multilateral barrier reduction. Trade liberalization must seek new channels if it is to be continued.

The idea behind reciprocity, the third GATT principle, is that the benefits of liberalization must be reciprocal or else the member states will find liberalization politically unattractive. Yet finding an acceptable formula to identify the reciprocal benefits of particular negotiations has become more and more difficult, especially since bargaining over nontariff barriers and special agricultural restrictions has taken on greater importance in successive GATT rounds. Few if any of these nontraditional tools of trade restriction produce effects that are easy to define, identify, or measure.

Take agricultural restrictions, for example. A central feature of the European Community is its highly protectionist Common Agricultural Policy. Like agricultural policy almost everywhere, it is a creature of domestic agricultural needs and pressures that were carefully reconciled in the negotiations leading up to its adoption and subsequent amendments. The European Community's attitudes toward the CAP, therefore, are not easily changed—as American negotiators have ruefully discovered in the Kennedy and Tokyo Rounds. While last-minute negotiations in the Tokyo Round did yield some liberalization in markets for agricultural products, the primary results of bargaining were on more pragmatic issues, such as CAP provisions for the height of support levels for certain farm crops and the working out of multilateral agreements to liberalize and stabilize international trade in meat and livestock and in dairy products (although similar agreement on cereals failed). At least it will be easier to measure the effects of changes in these provisions.

It remains to be seen how significant are the results of the Tokyo Round agreements on implementing the fourth GATT principle: control and surveillance of commercial policies other than tariffs. As noted above, negotiators initiated several codes of conduct designed to make the rules of good conduct in international trade more explicit and deviations from these rules more apparent. The code governing technical barriers to trade encourages openness in the procedures leading to the setting of product standards and discourages needless technical obstacles to trade. The code on government procurement is intended to open up government procurement contracts to international competition. The code on import licensing is meant to reduce this frequent bar to exports, particularly in developing countries. The customs valuation code is designed to ensure a more uniform and fair system for the valuation of goods for customs purposes. And the code on subsidies and countervailing duties promises new international discipline over agricultural and industrial subsidies and over domestic subsidies that distort historic trade patterns, and it bars the use of direct export subsidies. Some or all of these codes no doubt will be defied or conveniently reinterpreted by particular countries or interests, much as existing GATT rules have been violated repeatedly in times of pain or crisis. The hazards of violation are greatest, of course, during times of economic slack. But when the world economy turns upward again, little by little the codes may well acquire reality and greater respect. In this sense, the Tokyo Round may someday be regarded as a milestone on the road to liberalization (or more likely, as a barrier on the road to protectionism).

Unlike the design and implementation of the multilateral framework for trading relations which have occupied the time and energies of diplomats for decades, the search for a similar cooperative framework to assure efficient transfers of factors of production between nations has been underway for only a few years. Its beginning, indeed, can be marked with the publication of Jean-Jacques Servan-Schreiber's *The American Challenge* at the end of the 1960s, which sounded an alarm in Europe about the takeover of European industry by American multinational enterprises. Since multinational enterprises have become the major vehicle for international investments and capital flows, they now are regarded, with notable assistance from Servan-Schreiber, as primary agents of interdependence in the world economy.

The development of a rational framework to govern international investments and multinational enterprises is greatly handicapped by ignorance of their economic effects. Though anecdotal accounts of the behavior of multinational enterprises abroad and at home are widespread, there is surprisingly little information on which one can depend to predict the impact of particular investments on broad economic aggregates such as income, employment, the trade balance, or the balance of payments, either in the host country or at home. In general, recent research seems to suggest that the impact is not large, whether positive or negative, except in the case of particular sectors or regions where economic effects may be exaggerated because of the uneven distribution of economic activities within countries. But even these generalizations are shaky because we do not know, of course, what would have happened in the absence of international investments.

Despite the absence of this sort of information, significant progress has been made recently toward establishing a set of rules to guide the relationship between multinational enterprises and the governments of host and home nations. In 1976, for example, the OECD issued a "Declaration on International Investment and Multinational Enterprises" which sets forth guidelines for the conduct of multinational enterprises in host countries, but says little about the responsibilities of host governments toward the firms. Important discussions also are taking place at the United Nations and the

UNCTAD, where differences seem greater than at the OECD because of the diverse perceptions among developing countries about the impact of multinational operations in their home economies.

If the maximization of economic welfare is the objective, any comprehensive framework for the control of multinational enterprises should deal symmetrically with the obligations of firms and governments. It should spell out what good behavior means for the multinational enterprise, including the rule that firms not act to undermine the policies of host or home governments. It should, in turn, stipulate that governments treat multinational enterprises like they do any other national firm, rather than subjecting them to discriminatory and therefore distorting taxing, licensing, and regulatory requirements. It might in addition strive to harmonize tax, antitrust, and securities regulations as a means of removing other distorting influences on decisions about the location of international investments. And it should establish mechanisms to adjudicate disputes and to maintain surveillance of policies that do not seem to accord to the objective of maximum welfare.

The economic ideal is rarely achieved, however, because other criteria intrude so often on the decisions of interested governments. Because they are seen as agents of interdependence, multinational enterprises are regarded by most governments with suspicion—suspicion either that they are a trojan horse sneaking the interests of an alien government into the affairs of a "sovereign" state, or that they are agents of their own power, intent on "exploiting" the host economies without the accountability demanded of smaller national firms. Ongoing discussions meant to develop a new framework of control for international investments are likely, therefore, to be intensely political exercises at which suspicions of multinational enterprises are both the positive and negative poles of agreement—both the force that draws nations together to discuss the common "enemy" and the force that causes them to hold widely different views about how to control the worldwide activities of multinational enterprises. The prospect for further cooperative microeconomic policy-making of these sorts, therefore, is only mildly bright.

We shall discuss yet another sort of microeconomic cooperation—that of policies to assist the developing world—in the next chapter.

Conference Highlights

Coordinating Policies for Adjustment
Gerald M. Meier

The internationalization of markets has led inevitably to the desire for policy coordination, especially in response to changes in balance of payments and trading conditions.

Policy coordination can mean one of three things with respect to balance of payments adjustments. First, international policy coordination can be used as a means of forestalling or preventing balance of payments disequilibriums. If all nations perfectly coordinated their fiscal policies, monetary policies, wage policies, and commercial policies, a country would not need to endure the burden of adjusting its balance of payments. Second, international policy coordination can take the form of joint efforts to provide a more effective framework for the pursuit of international economic policies. The collective decision by member nations of the IMF to create Special Drawing Rights is an example of this type of policy coordination. And third, international policy coordination can be introduced for the purpose of easing the burden of adjustment to an existing balance of payments disequilibrium. Thus, rather than averting the problem of adjustment altogether, policies can be harmonized to distribute the burden of adjustment among nations in a more effective fashion.

All three types of policy coordination are illustrated in the agreements reached in Jamaica early in 1976 among members of the International Monetary Fund. They agreed first of all to legitimize existing exchange rate regimes and to charge the IMF with the responsibility to "exercise firm surveillance over the exchange rate policies of members." This is an important and new role for the International Monetary Fund. It acknowledges the fact that nations are fearful of freely floating exchange rates and that they will and do intervene from time to time in the exchange markets. But what kinds of intervention are legitimate, in the sense of promoting collective harmony, and what kinds should be outlawed? Clearly, the IMF has been handed a delicate task of multilateral surveillance.

The Jamaica accords also directed the IMF to "adopt specific principles for the guidance of all members with respect to those policies." The reason that this line was added to the directions of the IMF was to acknowledge the fact that domestic policies have profound effects on exchange rates, and that exchange rate surveillance cannot be made effective without some kind of discussion about and harmonization of domestic policies. Completely free and uncoordinated domestic policies would make the task of the IMF impossible.

Yet another aspect of the balance of payments adjustment problem addressed but not resolved at Jamaica is the problem of international liquidity. If a nation is suffering from a balance of payments deficit, it may adjust in several different ways: It can take domestic measures only, deflating the home economy; it can allow its currency to depreciate in the market for foreign exchange; it can impose restrictions on international trade or payments; or it can finance the deficit instead of adjusting if there is a lender of last resort in the system that will provide sufficient liquidity. Which choice a nation makes depends very much on world attitudes about international liquidity, a topic that has lost attention since the beginning of managed floating. A Keynesian wanting more expansion in the total system might very well argue that there is too little liquidity today, that to get to full employment around the world, there will have to be international deficit spending much as occurred in the Bretton Woods system prior to August 15, 1971.

My main point is that there are costs associated with adjusting balances of payments. We need to speed up the process of adjustment, but in ways that can distribute the burdens of adjustment between deficit and surplus countries more equitably.

The internationalization of markets also has prompted the desire to coordinate policy responses to the threat of imports. As the real conditions of international trade have changed—by which I mean the aging of traditional products, the discovery of new techniques and new products, and the growth of multinational enterprises—older industries have had to make way for new industries, and older countries have had to make way for new countries. But senile or depressed industries and older countries have not, as a rule, given up gracefully when their traditional comparative advantages have disappeared. Their typical reaction has been to seek protection of local markets and other forms of assistance in order to avoid adjustment.

Thus, every country has some kind of escape clause in its trade legislation designed to avert serious domestic injury when imports threaten. For the United States, it appears as section 201 of the Trade Act of 1974. Here is an example of its use: In 1976, almost 25 percent of the exports of the European Community to the United States were under some kind of protectionist review or investigation. That amounted to more than $4.5 billion in exports, enlarged no doubt because automobiles were being considered in that year. Other countries have followed similar paths to domestic escape clauses, and have come to rely more and more on orderly marketing agreements, voluntary export restrictions, and the like.

In addition, there is of course Article 19 of the GATT which allows member nations not to lower a tariff, or to increase a tariff that has been lowered, if lowering it would threaten serious injury to domestic industry. But in recent years, nations have bypassed Article 19 in favor of domestic safeguards because they regard the rule as too severe. It is too severe because a prior tariff concession must have been made in order to justify a market safeguard. Suppose, for example, a nation wishes to raise the tariff on product x, an important domestic product endangered by imports of x. It must raise the tariff against all producers of x, according to the most-favored-nation principle, and then only if it has made roughly equivalent concessions. Otherwise, countries injured by the tariff increase may retaliate by raising their tariffs or imposing quotas against the nation invoking Article 19. On the other hand, Article 19 is too lenient because it does not require a nation to undertake adjustment assistance, nor does it provide for degressive market safeguards, that is, safeguards such as tariffs or quotas that become more liberal in a short period of time.

I propose a return to the multilateral approach. A new Article 19 should be written which permits the use of a market safeguard only if imports have increased absolutely and then only if the safeguard is degressive and is tied to adjustment assistance. Countries now undertake market safeguards even if there is only a relative increase in imports. Under a revised Article 19, moreover, the justification for a safeguard might rest with an international review process, rather than (as it is now) with a process that risks a downward spiral of trade when important exporters, barred from the market by most-favored-nation treatment, retaliate in frustration. The protective safeguard should be degressive and adjustment assistance should be made available in order to speed up the process of moving resources out of depressed industries and into others.

The problem of adjusting to imports is, to a large degree, a problem of equity and fairness at the microeconomic level. It is the problem of textile workers in the South and of the costs of their dislocation. In a way, imports are like pollution or accidents. They are viewed as a nuisance, generated at significant cost in the process of producing something of value. The public policy problem is not one of reducing them to zero—any more than we wish to incur the costs of reducing pollution or accidents to zero—but one of finding the optimal amount of imports. Even Ricardo when he advocated repeal of the Corn Laws, recommended that it be done over a period of years by dropping the duty one shilling per quarter over a long period of time.

Nations fear free trade and freely floating exchange rates. They want safeguards against the costs of dislocation imposed by them. The problem is to bring the safeguards under multilateral review, thus accelerating the internationalization of institutions which has been lagging behind the internationalization of markets.

Treating Unemployment and Inflation
Robert Solomon

The most serious problems currently facing the industrial world are unemployment and slack economies, particularly in Europe and Japan. The good old days of the 1960s, when Europe was growing rapidly, seem to have gone away. In my view, the means of coping with these problems are known. They await someone of Keynes's persuasiveness, who can help the policy-makers act more wisely, both in the interest of their own countries and in full recognition of the new interdependence among nations.

In a way, the industrial world got itself into this fix in the first part of

the 1970s. Finding themselves in a bit of a slump, the major industrial countries adopted stimulative policies which expanded their GNPs 8 percent during a twelve-month period in 1972-73. That's a very rapid rate of expansion,
and it brought with it an enormous demand for raw materials which
boosted raw materials prices by the largest amounts in recorded history. In
addition, individual industrial countries failed to take into account the fact
that other industrial countries also were expanding rapidly. This lapse of a
sense of interdependence caused the exports of most countries to rise more
rapidly than expected, boosting aggregate demand still higher. Then, too,
this was the period when failure of the grain harvest in the Soviet Union led
to enormous grain purchases in the West, increasing food prices throughout
the world. Then at the end of 1973, OPEC quadrupled oil prices. The combination of these forces led to double-digit inflation in the industrial
countries.

The residue of that earlier period of excess demand is a wage-price cycle
going on in almost every industrial country. When prices rise so rapidly,
workers respond by demanding higher wages, sometimes with quite a lag.
Wages rise faster than productivity because it is expected that prices will
continue to rise at current rates, and prices continue to rise because wages
are increasing faster than productivity. And that spiral has just kept going,
despite the fact that there is no excess demand in any industrial country. It is
what many people call a cost-push phenomenon.

The increase in oil prices also had an income effect, of course. It has
been referred to as a tax, because higher oil prices diverted purchasing
power away from the buying of other products to the buying of oil. This
withdrawal of purchasing power from the system reduced incomes and con-
tributed significantly to the 1975 recession.

Recovery from the recession was simply inadequate. It petered out in
many countries (but not in the United States) in 1976, leaving considerable
slack, especially in the countries of Europe. Contrary to the confusing
public statistics, the German economy grew only 1 percent in the course of
1977; in both the second and third quarters of 1977, its GNP actually declined. Industrial production fell, moreover, in almost every European
country and in Japan during 1977.

Why did this recovery peter out? One reason is that policy-makers were
confronted with something they were not accustomed to: slack economies,
low capacity utilization, and unemployment on the one hand, and still rising
prices on the other. Unwisely, some countries adopted policies whose purpose and effect were to restrict demand, even though the cause of rising
prices clearly was cost-push rather than demand-pull. These, in my view,
were misdirected policies. In other countries that suffer from what I have
called fiscophobia, attempts were made to reduce budget deficits simply out
of a fear of deficits. These actions too, undermined the recovery. In still
other countries, the fear was of a different kind—that somehow any small

increase of government expenditure would aggravate inflation. Yet from this distance, with high unemployment and widespread excess capacity, it seems unlikely that a little extra expenditure would have produced significant inflationary effects. In my view, there is scope for expansion in Western Europe without inflationary danger.

What are the remedies for this situation? For a while, the most widely discussed remedy was the so-called locomotive approach to recovery. It suggested that the three largest industrial economies—Japan, Germany, and the United States—should undertake stimulative domestic policies in order to help pull the rest of the world out of recession. These three countries were chosen because of their size and because at the time the concept was formulated all three had relatively strong balance of payments positions. The idea was not only that these three should expand, but also that by taking the lead in expansion, they would make it easier for other countries, many of which had serious balance of payments problems, to take some domestic stimulative action.

The locomotive approach apparently has now given way to what is called the convoy approach, which sounds more sensible because it implies that all the industrial countries will simultaneously adopt more stimulative policies, though perhaps each one to a different degree depending upon its own particular circumstances. The United States, for example, now has less excess capacity, more inflation, and a weaker balance of payments than several other industrial countries. The convoy approach sounds to me like a good idea. If all the industrial countries expand together, each one will benefit through interdependence feedback effects from the impact of its own policies on others. Coupled with incomes policies to cope with the wage-price cycle, this approach of mutually reinforcing expansion is a good recipe for recovery.

The major beneficiaries of such policies, of course, will be the residents of the countries adopting them, where potential output and potential income now are being wasted. But there would be other very important benefits. Some would accrue to the developing countries and to the peripheral industrial economies, whose exports would expand. Another benefit would be reduction of demands for protection from free trade. The threats of protectionism which are all around us are, to a large degree, inspired by high unemployment and low use of industrial capacity—problems that coordinated expansion would help alleviate. And still another benefit of expansionary policies would be stimulation of investment spending. While low rates of investment have several explanations, the common element in every country where investment is low is a high rate of excess industrial capacity. I tend to believe that a necessary, if not a sufficient, condition for getting a higher rate of investment expenditures in the industrial world is to achieve a higher rate of capacity utilization.

Orchestrated expansion of the industrial economies also would influence exchange rates, and this takes me to another problem of interdependence. In Europe, this problem is referred to as the dollar problem. It is revealed mainly in the fact that the Swiss franc, the deutsche mark, and the Japanese yen have risen very sharply against the dollar in early 1978.

Why have these currencies appreciated so much against the dollar? One reason is the fact that the American inflation rate is higher than that of Switzerland, Germany, and Japan. Another, perhaps more important reason is that the European and Japanese economies have been slack in the past year, while the United States economy has expanded quite vigorously. In that situation, it is not surprising that American imports rose faster than American exports. Yet again, American oil imports went up by $10 billion or so in 1977, worsening even more the U.S. current account deficit.

Under ordinary circumstances, much of this American current account deficit would have been financed by private capital flows into the United States. Short-term interest rates were three to four percentage points higher here than in West Germany, a differential that usually causes capital to flow freely. But it did not respond to the interest rate differential, apparently because the expectations of further movements in exchange rates outweighed the effects of the interest rate differential. This is another example of economic interdependence: The American deficit developed partly because Europe and Japan adopted domestic policies which left their economies slack; this, in turn, led to the upward movement of those countries' exchange rates; and the appreciation of their exchange rates has, in turn, aggravated the stagnation of the economies of Europe and Japan. Thus, the need for stimulative policies becomes all the greater as exchange rates move up.

Should the United States take action to arrest the slide of the dollar? First, the United States should enact an energy program. Though such a program would not have an immediate balance of payments effect, it would certainly affect expectations and have important psychological effects. Second, we probably should *not* raise interest rates much higher for fear of killing off the U.S. expansion. That would make no one better off, including Europe or Japan. Third, we probably should *not* greatly expand our intervention in the foreign exchange markets. There are definite limits to how much exchange market intervention can affect exchange rates. If we learned anything in the 1960s and 1970s during the too frequent foreign exchange crises, it was that it is impossible for governments to hold an exchange rate when market forces are pushing it strongly another way. If the United States intervened strongly, moreover, I think it would not be long before the German monetary authorities phone the U.S. Federal Reserve and said, "please stop; you are undermining our monetary policy."

The one other suggestion I have seen in the press recently is that the United States should do as other countries do and finance its deficit abroad.

Thus, it is argued, we should issue securities denominated in foreign currencies as a way of financing the current account deficit. If my advice were asked, I would counsel against adopting that course. For one thing, it would make the problem look like a purely American problem, which it is not. It is a mutual problem of the United States and the other industrial countries. Also, the sale of American securities denominated in deutsche marks or Swiss francs would tend to push up interest rates in those currencies which would not be helpful either to further domestic expansion in those countries or to our balance of payments.

In conclusion, the exchange rate problem requires for its solution action on both sides of the oceans. The United States should enact an energy program and a more forceful antiinflationary incomes policy, while Europe and Japan, in their own interest, ought to expand their economies more rapidly.

Interdependence and Monetary Unification
Francesco Forte

Rather surprisingly, the flow of commodity trade back and forth between the United States and the European Community, though large in absolute quantity, represents a quite small proportion of aggregate economic activity in each of the trading partners. Europe's exports to and imports from the United States, for example, constitute only about 2 percent of the Community's gross domestic product (GDP), and America's trade with Europe is little more than one percent of its GDP. If these relationships are a proper measure of interdependence, then United States-European Community interdependence must be rather low.

Why, then, has there been so much discussion about the need of the United States, Germany, and Japan to behave as growth agents for the world—as international locomotives, as it were? The contribution of U.S. expansion to export demand in Europe, and hence to expansion of the European economies, cannot be so great if the transmission mechanism through exports has to do with a flow that averages only 2 percent of the gross domestic product. Nor should expansion of American exports to Europe be so important for U.S. aggregate demand. Rather, American and European expansion are important to each other, and to the world, through expansion of aggregate demand in other large economies induced by larger import demand originating in the United States and Europe.

The correct point of view is to look at the relationship between expansion of the GDP and imports, with expected exports acting as a constraint. For "weak-currency" countries like France, Italy, and the United Kingdom, which ran large balance of payments deficits in the period of the oil crisis, the possibility of expanding their economies is limited by the condition that their exports must expand at least as fast as their imports; otherwise, they will have unbearable current account deficits. Exports thus become a condition rather than a mere transmission mechanism of expansion. If one assumes a constant relation between growth of imports and growth of GDP (a presumption sometimes considered too optimistic), and a constant share of exports in world trade, clearly these countries can grow only at the average growth rate prevailing in the world. And, if they still have to redress the balance between imports and exports, either because of persisting deficits such as those of France, or because of requests by international monetary institutions to repay debts such as those on which Italy and the United Kingdom must act, they will have to settle for a slower rate of growth. A similar iron rule of limited growth applies to countries of the Third World and probably to the Communist countries. The constraint is reduced only to the extent investment flows fill the current account gaps.

So, if the United States achieves a high rate of growth which allows other countries to increase exports and consequently to reduce their constraint on imports, even weak-currency countries will be able to increase their rates of growth. The fact that weak-currency large nations are allowed to do so, of course, does not imply that they will be ready to do so. The United Kingdom is now moving toward expansion by fiscal action at home. Italy is not, however, because the effects of its large public sector deficit are being counteracted by restrictive monetary policy and by unfavorable investment prospects related to business and political factors. French expansion also is conditioned by monetary, psychological, and political factors.

It should be remembered, in addition, that the other two potential world locomotives, Germany and Japan, have planned relatively modest rates of growth: 3.5 percent for Germany and 5 percent for Japan. Germany's behavior is of paramount importance to growth in the other large European Community countries; Japan's matters only indirectly, European exports to Japan being only 0.3 percent of the GDP of the Community. The German government fears that if it expands demand too much, domestic prices will rise more rapidly, both because skilled labor may become more scarce and because its actions, in the absence of deutsche mark revaluation, may lead indirectly to the importation of more inflation from abroad. It seems obvious, then, that Germany should welcome deutsche mark revaluation in order to neutralize other nations' high price increases, and that it should not complain about dollar devaluation. Its concern about inflation also would be less, no doubt, if it thought other nations were equally concerned about inflation. Germany's left-of-center government is prudent in expansion because with the election period nearing, it is looking to voters on the right side of its electorate to help capture marginal areas. Quite the opposite is happening in France, where its center-right government has promised expansionary action because with the election period nearing, it is looking to voters on the left side of its electorate to help capture marginal areas.

The widespread problem in most economies is that they seem unable to cause expansion by stimulating an investment boom. Yet an investment boom is the only assured way to provide the new jobs and higher productivity needed in the longer run to combat inflation and improve employment.

According to a 1977 report (known as the McCracken Report) by a group of independent experts to the Organization for Economic Cooperation and Development, "the countries who should expand their demand first are those who have a high rate of unemployment, a low inflation rate, a favorable balance of payments, large reserves, and a solid financial reputation." If a country wants all of these conditions fulfilled simultaneously, it should not expand its aggregate demand first: the United States should be excused because of its unfavorable balance of payments; Japan, because it has the lowest unemployment rate among industrial countries and a considerable rate of inflation; Germany, because its unemployment rate, particularly among domestic workers, is the lowest in Europe (even if larger than before); France, because it has a large balance of payments deficit; Italy and the United Kingdom, because their international debts and inflationary rates are unusually high. If, on the other hand, one needs only one of the above factors to qualify for expansion, all countries should expand first, since all have either a surplus in the balance of payments, unemployment, a solid financial reputation, or what have you. The fact is that some need more expansion but can afford it less, while others can afford expansion more but need and care for it less.

I believe that the McCracken Report is wrong to have linked the rate of growth and the rate of price increase too closely. Under decreasing cost conditions, as now prevail in Europe, expansion creates better market forces, prevents bad sectoral planning, discourages distortive planning and protectionism, and increases financial reliability. It leads to higher productivity and higher profits. It need not lead to higher prices. The philosophy of expansion should not be "you first." Expansion should be simultaneously undertaken under a plan of coordinated monetary and fiscal actions.

The five-year plan of action recently proposed by President Roy Jenkins of the Commission of the European Community to speed up movement toward full economic and monetary unification within the Community, would, I submit, provide the necessary, if not the sufficient, conditions for greater order, growth, and stability in the economies of Europe, and thus in the world economy. The basic philosophy of the Jenkins plan traces back to the McDougall Report, for which I was a study group member.

According to this report, monetary unification requires for its success a set of fiscal transfers out of an enlarged European Community budget to the less developed regions in order to create additional investments, increased incomes, and improved balance of payments conditions at the regional level. It also requires other general public sector actions to foster market unification and to cope with some basic communitarian problems.

Transfers to less developed regions will stimulate additional private capital flows. Higher employment rates and higher productivity, together with international transfers, will increase per capita incomes of less developed regions, boosting regional and national tax revenues and therefore shrinking public sector deficits with the same levels of expenditure. With higher productivity, wages in these regions and nations will be able to stay closer to the Community's averages without undermining monetary stability or competitiveness, and with improved employment levels, stabilization policies and rules of monetary soundness will be accepted more easily.

Both the McDougall Report and another study with which I am associated suggest that a transfer to the less developed regions equivalent to 1 percent of the GDP of the rich member countries will have a very important effect on the degree of monetary unification, on the rate of economic growth, and on the risks of instability. A unified market within the European Community arising from monetary union will stimulate added investment and productivity and will create a basis for enlarging the Community. Monetary unification also will make the European Community a more effective partner of the United States in promoting coordinated growth and in sharing the benefits and burdens of world monetary coordination, which now rest entirely on the dollar.

Accelerating the rate of growth is a key Community issue. We cannot solve our unemployment problems, especially those involving young people and women, with a growth rate at today's level of 3.5 percent. Nor can we solve the present problems of excess capacity in the basic sectors without higher growth—sectors whose investments were planned under the expectations of higher growth before the oil crisis. This excess capacity creates national incentives for protectionism.

Thus, the European Community seems to be moving in the right direction by wishing to implement its five-year program of monetary unification. In the words of a recent Council document, "in its principles [the program], is eminently political and must be transferred into acts."

Japanese Roles in World Economic Stabilization
Makato Hara

One comes away from many international discussions with the impression that it is somehow evil to realize a surplus if your nation is not an OPEC member. While I recognize that the common view does have a measure of validity, I fear that it gives rise to the very wrong impression that Japan is the root of all evil.

Consider, first of all, the U.S. demand that Japan expand its economy and put its trade balance in the red, as we heard it, for example, at the recent trade talks. I feel, judging by the present condition of Japan's economy, that taking up a policy of economic expansion is absolutely imperative, and I would say that the Japanese government has been altogether too dilatory in taking proper economic countermeasures. Japan should take the initiative on its own, without having to be prodded by America. A reduction in the high trade surplus by increasing imports is desirable because it raises Japan's standard of living and keeps inflation in check. Japan ought to adopt such a policy in the best interests of the country and as a means of combating protectionism.

However, I am rather leery of the notion that Japan is morally obligated to alleviate the burden of the deficit nations and to shoulder part of that burden itself. I am leery of it because I think it incumbent on the deficit nations first of all to exercise discipline themselves, and I fear that this concept of sharing the burden can become the handmaiden of procrastination in dealing with one's own problems. I am skeptical of this simplistic approach, secondly, because the fundamental problem in global economics today is the staggering current account imbalance between OPEC and non-OPEC nations brought about by the raising of oil prices. Making that imbalance manageable will require great cooperation between all the oil consuming nations, as well as great efforts by each individual nation.

Incidentally, if Japan and West Germany were to actively promote economic expansion, on the one hand, their imports from other non-OPEC nations would increase, but on the other hand, oil imports would also increase. This is particularly true in Japan's case where we know from experience that raising industrial production 1 percent requires increasing oil imports 1.4 percent. That would further enlarge the OPEC trade surplus, and this growth in Japan's economy would be linked to more or less greater oil imports by other non-OPEC countries as they expanded exports. Consequently, even if the non-OPEC members' burden-bearing became a little more dispersed as a result of Japanese and West German expansion, the aggregate deficit, or to turn it around, the OPEC surplus, would be further swollen, unless the OPEC countries were to radically increase their imports. Clearly, our present world situation must be viewed in the context of low economic growth rates, and our future depends upon the development of new energy resources and the development of oil-saving technology.

My second point is about the present exchange rate structure, the international currency problem, and the decline of the U.S. dollar. The locomotive theory—the notion that the largest and strongest nations should expand in concert in order to help all nations recover from recession—is actually proposed as an alternative to the demand that surplus nations raise their exchange rates. Tactically, surplus nations are being offered the choice of economic expansion or higher exchange rates. But opinion is divided as to how well the current exchange rate system functions to regulate or to adjust the international balance of payments. One is tempted to conclude from the emergence of the deficit-sharing theory that people are skeptical about the ability of exchange rate movements to bring about needed adjustments. The present system is not a perfectly free float, and many obstacles exist that prevent the price mechanism from operating properly, including trade protectionism, foreign exchange controls, and downward stickiness of wages and prices. These factors inevitably make it impossible for the regulatory function to operate effectively.

It would be foolish, therefore, to depend exclusively upon exchange rate fluctuations as the means of adjusting imbalances of payments. Special national and international countermeasures are needed. National policies to control demand are playing and will continue to play an important role in regulating balances of payments.

A central element of the whole structure of foreign trade and payments has been the existence of an international or key currency. The key currency is still the U.S. dollar, as it has been for some time, and history has shown that under any kind of international monetary system whatever, fluctuations in the key currency dramatically affect the whole system.

It is only to be expected that America, whose foreign transactions make up a small percentage of her total economy, will show relatively little interest in exchange rate fluctuations. Moreover, under the current system, America can, as the key currency country, finance its deficits merely by making dollar credits to overseas accounts. It can do this because it bears no international obligation to convert dollars into gold, and it can do so no matter how big a trade deficit it runs up, so long as it does not worry about the depreciation of the dollar in the foreign exchange markets. Therefore, America is in an advantageous position. But there is a very big catch. The rapid decline of the dollar not only throws international transactions into confusion and instability; it also raises up the ugly specter of inflation in America as the cost of imported goods climbs, and has the particularly baneful effect of raising the price of oil.

Looking over the world economy, which is plagued by the energy crunch and a multitude of lesser evils, I am forced to conclude that there doesn't seem to be a currency system any more suitable than the present floating rate system, nor does there appear to be any currency that can take the place of the U.S. dollar. This means that trends in the American economy and in American governmental policy are the leading influences of the international monetary system. Thus, I am pleased with the policy of active exchange market intervention which the Federal Reserve has been implementing since the end of last year. I also think highly of the administration's efforts to pass a comprehensive energy bill which, among other purposes, will reduce the country's dependence on imported petroleum. More important still, I am heartened by announcements that the Federal Reserve

Board and other central elements of the American government intend to cooperate closely with the treasuries and central banks of other nations in the achievement of greater stability in the foreign exchanges and the world economy.

Notes

1. This section draws heavily on Marina v. N. Whitman, *Sustaining the International Economic System: Issues for U.S. Policy*, Essay No. 121, and on the studies cited there. Used with permission.

2. Gerard and Victoria Curzon, "The Management of Trade Relations in the GATT," in *International Economic Relations of the Western World 1959-1971*. ed. Andrew Shonfield, vol. 1, pp. 147-62.

New Tensions in
North-South Relations

The new interdependence surely is not limited to relationships among the
great powers and great economies of the world. While the conference focused primarily on the sources and effects of political and economic interdependence among the member states of the European Community, the
United States, and Japan, its self-consciousness about the links of these nations with the vast majority of the world's peoples and nations that are poor
was evident in the comments of virtually every conference participant. To
ignore these links is not only foolish; it is wrong.

The New International
Economic Order

Having agreed that North-South relations matter—morally, politically, and
economically—conference members nonetheless were quick to point out
that the South speaks not with one voice, but with many voices, each seeking some new kind of relationship with advanced industrial countries.
Montek Ahluwalia of the World Bank, for example, comments later in this
chapter on the numerous individuals and groups, some private and some
public, who have suggested changes of one sort or another in the organization of the world economy and in the methods used to reach decisions in international economic institutions. Rather than dismiss their pleas as discordant and inconsistent, however, Ahluwalia tries to explain them with the
help of a useful taxonomy developed originally by Bhagwati. The fact that
many proposals are contradictory, he argues, is the inevitable result of differing perceptions about the consequences of existing or proposed international economic arrangements. To demand that the South speak with one
voice is unreasonable in view of its fundamental ideological, methodologi-
cal, and national diversity.

To be sure, it is possible to summarize certain common themes that have
emerged from these often disparate and sometimes harsh demands for a
New International Economic Order (NIEO). The first is that the rich industrial countries should make larger transfers of resources and technology
to the developing countries of the world. Among the specific proposals
linked to this theme are: increased official development assistance; international commodity agreements which enhance the prices received by primary

producers, and increase their incomes; relief from burdensome external debts; larger shares of new allocations of Special Drawing Rights at the International Monetary Fund; more preferential treatment of developing country exports, especially manufactured goods exports, in the markets of industrial countries; liberalized transfers of technology; and more severe controls on the operations and profits of multinational businesses in developing countries.

The second recurring theme in demands for the NIEO is that the poor and nonindustrialized countries be excused from behaving in the same ways that the governments of industrial countries are charged with under terms of international laws and conventions. Trade preferences, technology transfers, and codes of conduct for multinationals clearly fall under this theme as well as that of resource transfer. Another illustration of this theme is the assertion by many petitioners from the Third World of the right to expropriate foreign-owned property within their national boundaries, without regard to international legal conventions on compensation.

A third common theme of NIEO proponents is that the decision-making machinery of the world order be revised to enhance the influence and power of developing countries. Their rights at the International Monetary Fund and the World Bank seem to be most on their minds.

Perhaps the more interesting question is not "Why does the South speak in many voices?" but rather, "How can so many voices give the impression of a common set of thematic demands?" The answer to the latter question takes us to the heart of a fascinating new set of relationships within the developing world itself—a set of relationships that seems to be on the verge of transforming North-South relations as well.

The developing world is composed of at least 140 states, each uniquely situated along the development path, each facing its own set of problems and opportunities. In order to simplify the task of analyzing their collective plight, observers frequently have distinguished between two types of developing countries: the nations of the Fourth World, consisting mainly of south Asia and most of Sub-Saharan Africa; and the countries of the Third World, consisting of nearly all Latin American and Middle Eastern nations and most of East and Southeast Asia.

Transfers versus Access

When broken down in this way, the nations of the developing world seem to have dramatically different needs and desires: those of the Fourth World want transfers of additional resources through either traditional foreign aid channels or newer means of debt relief; and those of the Third World want access to new economic opportunities, such as freer entry to the markets of the industrialized countries for their manufactured goods exports, readier use of modern capital markets, and heightened access to modern technology.

The nations of the Third World also want a substantially increased say in the management of the world economy, both to achieve status and to assure proper attention to their interests on a continuing basis. Thus, the Third World countries are motivated as much by political objectives as by economic ones.

These important differences between the objectives of the Third and Fourth Worlds have been reconciled politically by the readiness of leading Third World countries to champion the causes of poorer Fourth World nations. The petroleum exporting nations, for example, have known from the beginning that boosting the prices of energy fuels would seriously damage the economies of poorer states; to avert isolation in the developing world, they instituted programs of aid to other states and became steady advocates of development assistance and debt relief for impoverished countries. Other Third World nations, eager to establish themselves as regional leaders and interlocutors for the North-South dialogue, instituted similar programs of support for the demands of the Fourth World. Fourth World nations, in turn, have seen advantages to building bridges to the Third World whose rapidly growing strength reveals tested development models worthy of serious consideration.

Thus, a new alliance of Third and Fourth World nations has been formed, ushering in a new kind of dialogue between the North and South. To be sure, the emergence of the NIEO as a serious international issue can be traced primarily to the dramatic gains achieved recently by certain Third World countries. But its credibility as a serious basis for discussion between the North and South has been greatly enhanced by the bargain struck between the Third and Fourth Worlds, presenting the advanced countries of the world with the need to make constructive responses to the demands of impatient and newly powerful peoples the world over. Choosing not to accommodate seems risky, both because of political reasons and because of the possibility of it leading to their exclusion from vital sources of materials supplies, attractive investment opportunities, and markets for their expanding production—especially of sophisticated manufactured goods and technical services.

Europe's Response:
The Lomé Agreement

The European Community's response to demands for the NIEO is contained to a considerable degree in the Lomé Convention, on which Corrado

Pirzio-Biroli lavishes such praise in the conference highlights section of this chapter. It was concluded in February, 1975, between the European Community and forty-six (enlarged recently to fifty-two) developing states located in Africa, the Caribbean, and the Pacific (ACP states). It succeeded the Yaoundé Convention which the Community had negotiated with nineteen states before the United Kingdom had become a full member of the Community in 1973.

The Lomé agreement was of special importance for three reasons. The first is that it was the strongest evidence yet of the mounting readiness of developing countries to loosen their bilateral ties with former metropolitan countries and to multilateralize their international economic relations. The fact that the anglophile and francophile states could agree to negotiate collectively was a major development. Second, the ACP signatories to the agreement included some of the poorest developing countries in the world. While Africa is the least developed continent, the countries associated with the Community are among the least developed and least industrialized in Africa. Sixteen are on the United Nation's list of the twenty-five least developed countries.

The third reason for acknowledging its special importance is that the Lomé agreement included provisions for moving beyond traditional trade and aid policies—the standard bases of North-South economic relations of the past. It included more active forms of industrial, technical, and financial cooperation (Titles III and IV) than were usually followed even in colonial times, and it provided a commodity income-support system (Title II). The agreement allows duty- and quota-free access for ACP products to Community markets and nondiscriminatory most-favored-nation treatment of European exports to the ACP countries. Accordingly, the developing states that were signatories to the agreement do not have to grant the reverse preferences that were a major point of contention under the Yaoundé accord. The so-called Stabex mechanism helped to even out the export earnings of a dozen (recently expanded to eighteen) commodities on which the ACP states depended heavily to finance their development plans, and it extended special concessions to the least developed ACP member states. It even went a step further in the case of sugar, guaranteeing a market for ACP nations' output and indexing its price to domestic support levels within the Community. The agreement also provided development grants totaling nearly $4 billion through the European Development Fund.

Hailed by the Community's Commission as "a historical event," "a gleam of common sense in this world," and "a new model," and affirmed by official statements of many ACP states, the convention has nonetheless been criticized in Europe and elsewhere for several reasons. Among the criticisms that have been leveled are, first, that the provisions of the Lomé Convention are not generous enough. For example, it has been charged that the real benefits to be derived from the sections that govern trade in manufactured products are quite restricted as a result of severe rules of origin; that preferences granted to ACP agricultural products are not as liberal as they appear to be, because they are hemmed in by relevant provisions of the Community's Common Agricultural Policy; that the Stabex scheme is underfunded and needlessly narrow with respect to product coverage; that funding of the European Development Fund is inadequate; and that Title III on industrial cooperation is infeasible politically. Those who make these kinds of criticisms probably accept the notion that a complex mixture of special relations between groups of developing states and industrialized states is necessary, even though this entails the danger of a drift toward blocs. They no doubt believe also that the absorptive capacity of developing countries (of the ACP states, in this particular case) for additional assistance is positive and that the industrialized countries have an obligation (however motivated) to be more generous.

A second kind of criticism originates among those who believe that realization of the NIEO depends upon maintaining Third and Fourth World unity in the face of the industrialized nations. For this group, the Lome Convention is devisive, not because it has engineered larger transfers of economic resources to developing countries, but because it has done so in a way that undermines the political cohesiveness of all petitioners from the South. Even within the Lomé arrangements, they point out, the quality of the political relationships between the Community members and certain ACP states varies widely.

Finally, the Lomé Convention has been criticized as an important derogation of the principles of a multilateral liberal international economic system. Whether one is partial to the ideas of the "benign neglect" school or to those of the "benign intent" school (as explained by Ahluwalia), true believers will decry the degree to which the provisions of the Lomé agreement interfere with the benevolent influences of trade and investment flows on the development of poor countries. "Trickle down" lives, according to graduates of these schools of thought, and must not be allowed to dry up through well-intentioned but damaging interferences with the liberal market mechanism.

America's Response: A Liberal Order

In his statement to the conference, Isaiah Frank defended a significant variation on this liberal order theme, both as a matter of personal belief and as an "American view" on reform of the international economic relations of developed and developing states (see the conference highlights of this chapter). Rather than focusing almost exclusively on schemes that would have the effect of taking real resources away from developed states and giving them to developing nations—schemes that dominate the lists of demands for the NIEO—he made special note of opportunities for mutual gain. In particular, he noted the overwhelming importance of developing countries' exports as a source of purchasing power, not only raw materials and foodstuffs, but especially labor-intensive and technologically stable manufactured goods.

The policies that inhibit realization of the full potential of export earnings are in large measure the commercial policies of developed countries. In particular, tariff structures that now distort the location of early-stage processing of raw materials in developed countries should be altered to permit economic location nearer the raw materials, and protective tariffs and quantitative restrictions against competitive manufactures from developing countries should be eliminated in developed countries. The developing countries also would gain by reducing their own sometimes absurdly high protection against imports, which increasingly will inhibit mutually productive specialization among developing countries.

Alterations in existing structures of protection can lead to painful adjustments and losses for some previously protected producers, of course. Even David Ricardo, the ninetenth-century father of comparative advantage theory, acknowledged the presence of short-term adjustment costs in the process of achieving the longer-term benefits of international specialization. But until recently, according to Frank, the longer-term gains of efficient production were widely perceived to be much larger than the costs of attaining it. Now, he points out, the perception of gains may have faded somewhat, especially in Europe, and the assessment of costs may have risen as nations the world over strive for greater stability and social harmony. The theory of comparative advantage, according to Pirzio-Biroli, may not even have been meant to describe the trading relationships among countries as vastly different as the First and Fourth (or even the Third) Worlds of today. Even so, Frank clearly believes that the core of American policy toward the developing countries ought to remain in the liberal traditions of the past.

A second source of mutual gain for developed and developing states is from better management of the economies of the Western countries. As outlined in chapter 5, higher rates of employment, faster growth, and reduced price variability redound to the benefit of all nations, since their individual economies are linked inextricably one to another. Aggregate demand policies that take into account the influence of their effects on others are essential. Price stabilizing schemes that do not simultaneously have the effect of raising average prices also are important.

Though unmentioned at the conference, improved management of the global commons also holds the potential for substantial mutual gains. Overfishing, waste disposal, and shipping congestion all produce undesirable side effects which can be corrected by cooperative management of the oceans. Though still in the future, mining the deep seabeds may also yield significant benefits. Revenue may be raised as a by-product of efficient management of the oceans, permitting the beginnings of transfers through a world fiscal system.

In the longer run, efforts to enhance world food supply through financial assistance and transfer of relevant technology, and to raise the degree of competition for global corporations in world markets, also would greatly benefit peoples of all nations.

Frank's emphasis of reforms that involve more than a simple transfer of resources from one nation to another seems not to be meant to minimize the importance of aid transfers. Indeed, his interesting dialogue with Ahluwalia reveals his readiness to endorse transfers, especially to Fourth World developing states that have not yet progressed sufficiently to benefit equitably from the gains of international specialization. Rather, he seems to be saying two things: First, that the focus of negotiations ought to be shifted away from those areas which by their nature create tension and conflict, toward those areas from which all negotiating parties might reasonably expect some positive form of gain; and second, that some reforms of the international economic order that have been proposed by groups representing the developing world are inefficient means of arranging transfers from the rich to the poor. In his view, commodity agreements that have as their principal purpose the elevation of average price above its equilibrium value are notoriously poor vehicles for redistributing world resources.

Clients, Transfers, and Markets

If Frank's preferences fairly represent the basis of American policy toward demands for the NIEO—and the author tends to think that they do—then it is interesting to compare them with those implied for Europe which serve as the basis of the Lomé Convention. The first impression one gets from comparing European and American responses is of the heavy emphasis on resource transfers in the European response—more aid, income-raising commodity agreements, special trade preferences for the poorest states—and of the emphasis in the American response on the creation of new market opportunities, especially for developing countries well along the development path.

The explanation for these differences probably lies in two quite basic differences in the political economies of Europe and America. The first is that these centers of advanced industrialism have served two rather dif-

ferent client groups in the rest of the world. The developing world with which
the Europeans have been primarily concerned is composed of former colonial
states in Africa and south Asia, the majority of them part of the Fourth
World. To focus especially on responses that generate resource flows to them
much more than exposed market opportunities makes a good deal of sense.
These flows, of course, have been generously supplemented by bilateral
economic and military assistance initiated by individual metropolitan countries of Europe still retaining close ties with former colonies.

The Third World nations relating most directly with America, on the
other hand, are much more ready for the winds of market competition; and
America's concentration on the creation of new trade and investment opportunities for these nations, and on technological transfers, also makes
sense. To say that one strategy is better than another, as was said by some
conference participants, is to miss this fundamental difference in the geo-
political relations of advanced states with the rest of the world.

The other possible source of differences in European and American
responses to demands for the NIEO may lie in their basic differences in
political philosophy. The views of most politicians about how the international economy should be managed are, not unexpectedly, an extension of
their views about how their domestic economies should be managed. Countries that place a low value on their bureaucracy tend to favor open international economies with minimal barriers to the free flow of goods and
capital. Countries with strong centralized bureaucratic controls over their
domestic economies, on the other hand, favor the use of bureaucratic controls to manage international payments. It probably is safe to say that
Americans still place more trust in market solutions to problems of resource
allocation than do the Europeans as a group. They respect the bureaucrats
less than do Europeans. Thus, even for an entirely similar set of client
states, one can suppose that Americans and Europeans will choose
marginally different means of organizing interstate economic relationships—reflecting the Americans' dependence more on markets, the Europeans' dependence more on bureaucrats, to assist poorer nations to change
and grow. One sees evidence of these philosophical preferences in the
development strategies of the industrial powers.

Conference Highlights

Needs and Hopes of the Developing World
Montek S. Ahluwalia

I am entrusted with the frightening responsibility of speaking for the largest
proportion of humanity—the world's poor. I cannot hope to do credit and

justice to everyone's views on the NIEO, of course, as there is really an extraordinary outpouring of works (of varying scholarship) on the subject. Instead, I will try to describe the context in which North-South tensions have arisen, and then I will discuss a few key issues now tending to dominate negotiations over the NIEO.

In a recent book entitled *The New International Economic Order: The North-South Debate*,[1] Jagdish Bhagwati identifies four different perceptions of the developed world's relationship with the developing world in the existing international economic order. He calls these perceptions "benign intent," "benign neglect," "malign neglect," and "malign intent," and suggests that opinion in the developing world is shifting toward the gloomier perceptions. Let me explain what I think he means by these views of the world.

The benign intent view once anchored the colonial philosophy that the North was engaged in some kind of civilizing mission to the developing world. With the end of colonialism, this view reflected itself in the humanitarian arguments for foreign aid and foreign investment which were seen as mechanisms for assisting poorer countries to receive the benefits of modern ideas and newer technologies. I think it is fair to say that this view has lost popularity even in the developed countries. Few people now put it forward as the primary feature underlying North-South economic relations.

The benign neglect view of the existing order essentially holds that the links of the developing nations to developed countries produce beneficial results for the poor without any special need for international policies aimed at helping poorer countries or poorer people. The existing international system is seen to be more or less automatic and fundamentally benign. It allows nations to do well for themselves and to grow to their fullest potential without much need for help. In former times, this is a view that certainly was shared by very large numbers of people, especially in the developed countries. While it continues to have many adherents, this view, too, has waned. Fewer people now feel that the existing system, left to itself, can provide an environment that is in some sense equitable and capable of promoting expansion. This loss of faith applies not only to the international system as it affects North-South relationships, but also to North-North relationships.

The third view is of malign neglect. It suggests that the existing links between rich and poor nations have unintended adverse consequences on less developed countries. Some economists argue, for example, that through the establishment of enclave production sectors in developing countries, large foreign companies distort domestic labor markets, adversely affect domestic consumption patterns, create unrealistic attitudes toward technology, and so on. The malign neglect view, therefore, is a logical successor to disenchantment with the benign neglect view, in which the outcomes of international linkages also simply happen without intent; but the results are bad rather than good for the host countries.

Finally, those who hold to the malign intent view see distinct harm being done to developing countries as a result of the operations of the existing order, and they believe these outcomes to be intended rather than unintentional. The obvious examples, chosen especially by Marxist and New Left writers who see the world in this way, are some of the operations of multinational corporations that deliberately create greater dependence on rather than liberation from some forms of colonialism, and frequently interfere in the domestic political process.

An important aspect of the background in which North-South tensions have arisen is the shift from benign to malign views by many people, especially in the developing worlds. Official opinion seems to be shifting from benign neglect to the idea of malign neglect, though not necessarily to malign intent. Those who now subscribe to the malign intent view, by and large, tend to be unofficial rather than official representatives of developing country opinion.

I should mention in this connection that a good deal of the intellectual activity associated with the NIEO is quite radical, calling not only for a delinking of the developing from the developed world, but also for a complete transformation of the social and political relations within developing countries. Since this conference is meant to explore international linkages, I will not deal with the problem of transforming national social and political systems within countries. That is a topic for another conference.

Even if we restrict ourselves to the points of view in the developing world, we find enormous diversity. It is a mistake to look for unity among such a vast profusion of official views. The fact is that there are different points of view, and some of them are not consistent with others. Yet all views stress the inadequacy of existing results. Virtually every observer wishes somehow to restructure the existing order in ways that will deliver more benefits to the less developed countries. We must not use the fact that there are discordant voices speaking for the developing world to hide the very substantial agreement on the need for some reform of the existing system.

How ought we appraise the issues raised in demands for a New International Economic Order? What questions should we ask of ourselves in order to sort out useful from harmful specific proposals for reform? Here are four questions that may help your thinking about the issues: First, are the issues now under discussion, broadly speaking, the right issues? Second, have the demands made by developing countries been well articulated and are they, as it were, sensible? Third, what priorities should be attached to each leading issue, and are these priorities likely to be the same for developing and developed countries? Finally, what strategies have developing countries employed to pursue these issues?

The issue that developing countries invariably put at the top is resource transfer. By resource transfer I mean not only the quantity and quality of development assistance flows, but also the rescheduling or cancellation of debts owed by developing countries to developed ones or to international institutions. Both kinds of transfers confront a rather basic disagreement between giving and receiving countries about the motivation for resource transfers: people from the developing world harboring a malign neglect view have a strong desire to demand aid as compensation for past wrongs rather than to simply request it; people in developed countries, by contrast, who still view the world from the perspective to benign intent or benign neglect, see aid as charity. Inevitably, it is a tension-filled issue.

Compounding the difficulty, there has been a distinct decline in the willingness of developed countries to provide assistance as measured by the value of assistance flows relative to the gross national products of donor countries. Proponents of the benign intent and benign neglect perceptions emphasize the importance of increasing resource transfers as a means of improving conditions in the less developed world. But practice has fallen short of promises. This has undoubtedly affected the credibility of the benign views of the existing economic order.

A second important issue raised in the debate over the NIEO is that of trade. It is in two parts. One is the issue of commodity stabilization on which there has been enormous attention lavished and much noise generated. The other is about the export of cheap manufactured goods by less developed countries, goods made primarily with their abundant labor resources. In my view, the wrong priorities have been assigned in the debate to these two means of exporting. There is no question in my mind that the issue of market access for manufactured goods is much more important. Yet commodity stabilization schemes have been pushed so hard by the less developed countries, despite internal inconsistencies, that they have acquired a symbolic value that goes beyond ordinary economics. It is possible that the emphasis on commodity schemes has distracted attention in the developing world from the much greater long-run potential of obtaining access to markets for manufactured goods.

Let us recognize, even so, that protectionist sentiment has risen recently in the developed countries. This fact may be the temporary result of a fairly slow recovery from recession in most of the advanced nations, but who is to know whether it is temporary or not? It seems to me that the developed countries have a clear responsibility not only to curb the rise of protectionism, but also to reduce the existing levels of protection through the so-called orderly marketing arrangements and voluntary export restrictions.

The roles of multinational corporations in developing countries constitute the third major issue in the debate. The experience of the last five years probably has convinced almost everybody that some kind of code of conduct for multinational corporations is necessary. This is an area to which developed and developing nations could come as equals to negotiate a code that is really sensible and fair.

Finally, the issue of food security requires very much more attention. The experience of 1972-74, when bad harvests in successive years threatened national and international calamities, convinced many people that the existing international economic order does not adequately provide for efficient responses to unanticipated crises. Food supplies are essential to national survival, and food cannot be regarded simply as another good in international trade. Some new means of food security operated in an internationally cooperative manner must be found.

Though short, this list of leading issues in the debate over the NIEO contains extremely complex questions demanding prompt and thoughtful answers. The answers to these questions, moreover, may yield mutual benefits to developed and developing countries alike. Because of this possibility, the developed countries ought to take much larger initiatives in finding a mutually satisfactory design for the New International Economic Order.

Responses by the European Community
Corrado Pirzio-Biroli

An American scholar has said that foreign policy leaders schooled in the old arithmetic of national security will have to learn the new formula of economic interdependence. Unfortunately, both sides of the North-South conflict feel that true interdependence, however formulated, is very difficult to swallow. The industrial countries feel that their dominant position, their wealth, their very system, is threatened by agreeing to discuss North-South questions. The developing countries resent their present lack of representation in decision-making forums as well as the little weight given to income distribution questions by the present world system. Both contenders favor a system granting stability and forecasting ability to the international economy, conditions that the Bretton Woods system succeeded very largely in achieving. But they do not agree on the role of free trade. The reason is probably that the law of comparative advantage was never meant to apply to widely unequal partners. The Bretton Woods system, moreover, was an agreement designed by a few more or less equal partners, and the world has changed since.

No dialogue is possible between partners who are beset by fear like the developed countries, or by hostility like the developing countries, or by the isolation of the Eastern bloc which is completely outside the dialogue. The isolation of the Eastern bloc appears insurmountable. So, negotiations to reshape the present order will have to go on between the West and the developing countries for the time being.

The difficulty at this time, unlike the period when the Bretton Woods system was formed, is that there is not one leader who can facilitate the finding of solutions through his sheer strength. A new order will have to be fought inch by inch, taking, say, a decade.

In 1976, the Trilateral Commission observed that European initiatives are "the most effective route" on issues concerning North-South relationships. There are several reasons why this is so. First, as a civilian power, the European Community has an interest in laying stable foundations for world peace without the need to use weapons. A precondition to peace is greater equality among nations. This implies the need for differentiated rules, because nations are unequal economically and politically. These rules cannot be imposed from above, but must be negotiated if they are going to last. And the Community has shown some talent in this respect.

Second, the European Community is so dependent on raw materials—five times more so than the United States and ten times more so than the Soviet Union—that it is forced to play the interdependence game. It has no choice.

Third, the European Community is ideologically a flexible international actor, as the varying composition of its governments shows; therefore, it provokes less suspicion among developing countries.

Fourth, European institutional arrangements are a marvelous training ground for conducting controversial negotiations in a wider context. They are not very secretive (unfortunately so, we say at times); everyone knows what they are discussing. But in a way, this fact creates less suspicion on the side of developing countries. They know what is being discussed in the Council.

Last, but not least, the Europan Community member states felt, unconsciously perhaps, that responding positively and jointly to North-South issues could be a means of counting more in world affairs; a way, as it were, to reclaim lost sovereignty.

The Community's actions concentrated first on regional agreements with neighboring countries which were increasingly contractual in type and global in nature. We took this approach because we believe that a general system of trade, aid, commodity stabilization, industrial cooperation, and common institutions to discuss these issues is a better way to cooperate with developing countries than splitting up the issues. We chose to work first with the countries closer to us, that is to say, those which are part of what might be called a European monetary area. The approach was then extended to several Commonwealth countries when the United Kingdom joined the Community. Extending it further would jeopardize it; a pilot scheme must be small. An experiment with something as new as stabilization of export commodities is riskier at a world level. Making it initially small permits us to propose it at a larger level if it works.

The pièce de résistance of our regional approach has been the Lomé Convention. There are several features of the agreement that may be regarded as "new," in the NIEO sense. The first is that the developing partners—the fifty-two African, Caribbean, and Pacific countries that are associated with the Community—enjoy free access to Community markets without any reciprocity. The first time this concept was implemented was through the General Scheme of Preferences of the Community. But it is new in the sense that it covers all products of the partner states. Ninety-nine percent of their exports enter our market freely.

Second, the ACP partners are allowed to discriminate against the Community, provided it is in favor of other developing countries. We feel that cooperation among developing countries must be promoted. Third, there is a stabilization scheme covering eighteen primary commodities which acts as a sort of insurance policy that pays off in bad years. The developing countries have very great difficulties planning their development when the proceeds of raw material exports fluctuate enormously. The stabilization scheme is meant to solve part of that problem. Commissioner Cheysson said that this scheme could be likened to recognition of the right of unemployment and sickness benefits for workers in the developing countries.

Perhaps the most revolutionary aspect of the Lomé Convention is the commodity agreement on sugar. The European Community has agreed to guarantee purchase of 1.4 billion tons of sugar annually from its partners at prices based on those which the Community negotiates for its own sugar at the Community level. So, in fact, there is some form of indexation built into the guarantee because prices of Community-produced sugar tend to go up with inflation.

Fourth, the Lomé agreement provides for an industrial development center where contact may be made between entrepreneurs from Europe and the partner states. There is, in addition, provision for financial and technical cooperation of $4 billion, mostly in the form of grants, to smooth the agreement and to help in development cooperation.

Fifth, the Lomé Convention identifies twenty-eight partners as least developed, and provides them with more aid and better returns from the stabilization scheme. Thus, the agreement breaks new ground by treating the least developed countries differently.

Finally, there are jointly managed institutions. Stability requires not only a contract, but also an institutional mechanism which forces all parties in the agreement to try to solve problems that may arise during the period of the convention. The advantage of a global agreement of this kind is that it encourages cooperation beyond traditional areas of simple financial cooperation.

I believe that the Lome Convention is a political event of international significance, perhaps the greatest event for the Community since the creation of the Community itself. But it is not a total answer to demands for a new international economic order. It is, rather, a pilot scheme which must be monitored and improved upon as time goes by. This is why the European Community and its partners are planning to enter into negotiations in September, 1978, which will lead to a modified agreement for another five-year period.

The Commission of the European Community tends to support the view that the new interdependence among nations requires that we strengthen decision-making power at the world level. If this is so, the reinforcement of political economic cohesion of regional groups seems to be essential as a first step in cutting down the effective number of partners engaged directly in collective decision-making on truly international matters. Establishment of the European Community, for example, made possible the Kennedy Round of trade negotiations. Had we negotiated separately, there would have been so many differences of position between, say, Germany and France, that the likelihood of successful negotiations would have been greatly reduced.

Responses by the United States
Isaiah Frank

There is a strange asymmetry in the dichotomy between North and South. There is a North, but in my view there is no South. There is a North in the sense that a group of about twenty countries are at about the same level of economic development. The gap between, say, Italy and the United States or the Scandinavian countries is fairly narrow. It is perhaps one to two. Among developing countries, by contrast, the gap between, say, Mali and Brazil is more than one to ten. Brazil and Italy have greater similarities in economic aspects than do Brazil and Mali. In political terms, every country in the North is a parliamentary democracy. Among the developing countries, one has a very wide range of political organizations, ranging from, say, India, a parliamentary democracy today, to Uganda. I therefore think that when we incautiously lump the South together, we are using shorthand to deal with a problem of great diversity and great complexity.

Arnold Toynbee once wrote that when the history of the latter half of the twentieth century is written at some future date, its greatest achievements will be seen not as technological ones, such as the conquest of space and the revolution in communications, but as profound social changes that have occurred in our lifetime, especially acceptance of the proposition that progress is possible for all mankind, regardless of race or previous condition of colonial servitude and, most important, that we must act on that proposition. That is a revolutionary idea.

I believe there is no disagreement between North and South on the idea that progress is not only possible, but necessary, in the South. Our differences relate, by and large, to the means of achieving progress in poor countries; that is to say, the policies that need to be followed if developing countries are to realize their full potentialities.

According to David Morawetz, the author of a remarkable little book published by the World Bank called *Twenty-five Years of Economic Development, 1950 to 1975*,[2] the postwar record of progress in the developing world under the existing economic order is truly impressive. In the quarter-century 1950 to 1975, the average per capita income of the developing countries grew by 3.4 percent per year in real terms. That was more rapid growth than they had ever achieved before and more rapid than the now developed countries had experienced in any comparable period in their history. Moreover, this growth was not a statistical artifact, nor was it confined exclusively to economic dimensions. Increases in life expectancy that took a century in the industrialized countries have been achieved in the developing countries in two or three decades. Tremendous progress in other indices of real welfare, such as the eradication of communicable diseases and the spread of literacy, also has been broadly shared.

To be sure, averages can conceal as much as they reveal, and there has been a wide diversity of experience among developing countries. One group of countries has grown rapidly, but has shared the benefits of growth quite unevenly with different groups of citizens. Another much smaller group, also quickly growing, has been much more even-handed in the distribution of benefits. And still a third group experienced disappointingly slow growth and a relatively unequal distribution of such increments of income as became available. The latter group includes a large part of south Asia and some of the poorer parts of Africa, which constitute about 40 percent of the developing world.

But I think we can be optimistic. Things turn around rather quickly. No country should be written off. In 1950, Taiwan was recovering from occupation and war. The Korean peninsula was newly divided and at war; the situation was grim. Yet today both of those countries are among the most successful of the developing countries. One economist, Ben Higgins, wrote in 1959 that if Libya can be brought to a stage of sustained growth, there is hope for every country in the world. Well, the latest edition of the *World Bank Atlas* indicates that Libya is one of the fastest growing countries in the world.

What are the problems? Really, if I may permit myself an oversimplified dichotomy, there are two kinds of problems that developing countries face; one set is internal and the other external. The internal problems are problems of this kind: is the country giving sufficient support and encouragement to agriculture? It is a rare developing country, except for the very special case of the OPEC countries, which without real progress in the agricultural sector, can achieve overall economic progress. What is happening in terms of expenditure of government funds in those countries? Are they being directed to the basic needs of the poorest parts of the population as well as looking to the future to increase the capital stock and productivity at some later date? What about taxation? Is there an efficient system of taxation and is its structure equitable? What about stimulating the entrepreneurship existing in many developing countries? Are controls stifling the initiative of the people? What about the domestic policy? Does it impinge on the foreign trade performance of the country?

These are critical internal economic problems. The new international economic order is not focused on these problems, however, despite the fact that in my view and, I think, in the U.S. view, these are the critical problems of developing countries. The NIEO is focused on a collection of other problems.

One problem on which it has been focused has been the centerpiece of demands for change by developing countries: the idea that we should create a common fund to support a so-called integrated commodity policy. I agree completely with what Mr. Ahluwalia has just said—that the stress on this particular aspect of international economic relations is a case of misplaced priorities.

A second focus of attention has been the multinational corporations. On this issue too, I hasten to say that although there are problems with multinational corporations, I think they have been vastly overstated. The evidence that the multinational is not the root of all evil is contained in the simple fact that the very developing countries that most loudly and stridently denounce the multinational corporations are often the same ones that are going to great lengths to attract them.

In my mind, the key external issue is trade policy. What is done with respect to trade policy will overshadow what is done in all other fields. I'd like to say a word about each of these three policies: commodities, multinational corporations, and trade.

One of the reasons that the developing countries have placed such high priority on the commodity problem is that commodity policy is perceived as an instrument for the achievement of resource transfers from North to South. The NIEO, in its treatment of commodity policy, recognizes that commodities are confronted with two problems. One is the instability of commodity prices, and the other is the alleged adversity of the terms of trade for exporters of primary commodities. By that I mean that over time, it is claimed, the prices of exports of primary commodities fall in relation to the prices paid for imports into the developing countries.

There is perhaps no doctrine that has so colored the thinking of the South about the inequities of the present international economic order as this view on the terms of trade. Yet the facts don't support this view. The UNCTAD recently assembled a group of experts, including a preponderance of experts from the developing world, to investigate the terms of trade issue. They concluded that there is no evidence of any generally adverse movement in the terms of trade for primary products. One has to look at commodities one by one.

The U.S. view, which is shared by at least several members of the European Community and also by Japan, is that commodity arrangements which are designed to raise the prices of commodities above what market levels would dictate, in the long run are inefficient ways of transferring resources. They are not experiments in which the United States will participate.

I suppose the most dramatic example of a price-raising resource transfer is the OPEC countries' commodity arrangement on oil. By raising the price of oil, the OPEC countries imposed on India, Pakistan, and many of the poorest developing countries an additional oil bill of about $11-12 billion annually, a sum just about equal to the total annual transfers of official development assistance from North to South. Resource transfers through this particular device are hardly a way of achieving equity in the international economic system.

Moreover, the division between South and North does not coincide with the division of primary commodity production in the world. Indeed, the North is a bigger exporter of commodities than the South.

The U.S. view on this issue is that one should follow a case-by-case approach. Even so, the new administration in Washington sees a mutuality of interests in the negotiation of stabilization agreements, and has, after at least twenty years, joined the tin agreement. It has joined the coffee agreement. And it has signed the international sugar agreement, despite the European Community's decision not to sign and to deal with sugar matters instead on a special basis with the ACP countries.

The principal complaint of the developing countries about multinational corporations is that this particular vehicle for the transfer of resources from North to South has many adverse consequences. It smothers local entrepreneurship. Instead of bringing in capital, it borrows locally. It manipulates intracorporate pricing to minimize the payment of local taxes. It stimulates inappropriate consumption patterns. It intrudes into local politics, supporting oppressive regimes. It introduces technology that is inappropriate to the resource endowments of developing countries. It charges too much for the technology, and then often attaches restrictive conditions to its use.

The prevailing view in the United States is that the analysis of this problem, and much of the rhetoric surrounding it, has not caught up with what has happened over the last ten years. Take the natural resource field, for example. In this field, the developing countries have widely nationalized the operations of multinational corporations, unbundling much of what the multinationals do by adopting so-called service contracts rather than permitting them any longer to hold an equity position. Now they sell their management services, their technology, their marketing facilities, and the rest. Whether this is better or worse for the developing countries or multinational companies is uncertain. But I have heard at least one multinational in the extractive field say that its income is much higher from these new arrangements, which, to be sure, give the developing countries a greater sense of control and sovereignty. The multinationals seem much more happy with them, even though these arrangements are the result of "expropriation."

As for the manufacturing field, developing countries have shown themselves to be increasingly sophisticated in negotiating the terms of entry for multinational corporations, in monitoring their performance, and in maximizing the gains that remain within the developing countries themselves. These changes have taken place gradually within the last decade, creating a situation today that is vastly different from the one Hans Singer called neocolonialism in the early fifties, a term that in many ways crystallized the views still held by many intellectuals and ideologues of the developing world. The people to whom Mr. Ahluwalia referred—the technocrats and government officials—are fully aware of the changes that have taken place.

The developing countries and the United States do not agree on what should be done now. The less developed countries put more faith in what a sweeping code of conduct would accomplish than the United States does. Furthermore, the less developed countries see a code of conduct as setting down principles, constraints, and guidelines for the multinationals, whereas the United States sees such a code as also including guidelines and constraints for the behavior of host and home countries. The United States prefers a more balanced arrangement, modeled after the set of voluntary guidelines that were adopted by the OECD countries only about a year ago to govern the operations of multinational corporations.

Let me conclude with a word about trade policy. The importance of trade policy completely overshadows the benefits of aid and other capital flows as a source of foreign exchange for the so-called non-oil-producing developing countries. Last year they exported something well over $100 billion. Since their exports have grown during the last six years at the rate of 8 percent or 10 percent a year, one year's annual growth in exports by the non-oil-producing developing countries almost equals the total of their receipts of official development assistance.

It also is important to stress the changing character of the exports of the less developed countries. Today, 40 percent of their exports are of manufactured products, and the proportion is growing rapidly. Since 1973 moreover, the growth of exports of the developing countries has outpaced that of the developed world.

What we are seeing is a rapid and revolutionary transformation, shifting comparative advantage in favor of the developing countries in two major sectors: those industries that use relatively large proportions of labor, and those industries characterized by technological stability. The principal policy issue that the North is going to face over the next ten or fifteen years is whether or not to continue to provide market access to the exports of developing countries which use for their production the one resource they all have in abundance, namely, inexpensive labor. This is the issue on which the success and continued progress of developing countries will depend.

I believe it is going to be difficult to maintain open access, for the following reason. A fundamental premise of liberal trade policy is that the long-term gains in efficiency and output obtained from international specialization and foreign trade exceed short-run transitional costs incident to the disruptions, dislocations, and instabilities of reallocating resources. Even David Ricardo, who first formalized the doctrine of comparative advantage, acknowledged this potential offset.

There is some feeling that this tradeoff between long-term gains from trade and short-term transitional costs may be shifting, at least in perception. I sense that the marginal value of additional real incomes is diminishing, especially among Europeans. If this is true, then the gains from trade, though as large as ever, may be valued less than before. Transitional costs, moreover, may be larger, and, for whatever size they are, less tolerable today as countries and societies put a greater weight on stability and social harmony, and are less willing to see concentrated adverse effects on particular segments of economies and societies.

The big issue for the future is how we are to reconcile the very great mutual advantages that come from open international markets with the costs of achieving them. This is not a zero-sum game, such as resource transfers are, in which a country parts with resources and gives them to somebody else. The great thing about trade is that you don't have to appropriate the benefits through the legislatures. One country doesn't gain at the expense of the others. There's mutual gain. But there are many political and economic realities to be faced in trying to maintain those open markets which are important to us but even more critically important to the developing countries.

One of the critical determinants of our ability to maintain open markets is how wisely we deal with the problems of unemployment and inflation at home. If we can maintain high levels of employment without excessive price increases, I think our willingness to maintain open markets will be very much greater. Domestic and foreign economic policy cannot be separated; healthy domestic economies make it far easier for us to follow policies that are conducive to the growth and development of the Third World.

Commentaries

Pirzio-Biroli: I have a few points of disagreement with Isaiah Frank.

First of all, I agree with him that many less developed countries have been growing rapidly. But the problem is the gap that has been growing between developed countries and a large number of developing countries, rather than their growth performance. It is differences in levels of living that are the problem. And to deal with these differences, we need a cooperative development policy with the Third World capable of applying instruments of development to these differences. The Community has tried to do this.

I agree with Dr. Frank that trade is the key issue and that the developing countries have assigned too much emphasis to commodity arrangements financed with a common fund. But the developing countries are pessimistic about the willingness of the developed countries to open their markets, the more so since duties have gone down but nontariff barriers have gone up for several products. Seeing little hope there, the developing countries are trying to get things moving in another field, which is the field of commodities. Their choice of emphasis really is the result of protectionist sentiments in the developed countries.

I agree with Dr. Frank also that 40 percent of the total exports of developing countries now are manufactured goods. But this has been partly the result of working of retail houses from the West, and he did not mention intrafirm trade. In fact, intrafirm trade now accounts for one-third of the total trade of developing countries. So the fact that 40 percent of their exports are manufactured products may overestimate the degree of benefit they receive.

The European Community agrees with the United States that commodity agreements are a poor way to transfer resources. But oil is a poor example. The price of oil picked up because it had gone down in constant terms during the fifteen years preceding 1973. Had it not been depressed, of course we would have transferred resources earlier; but then we would have used less energy. In fact, the price today probably corresponds more to equilibrium supply and demand conditions than it did when the oil multinationals were deciding what the price of the commodity should be.

Concerning multinationals, I agree with Dr. Frank that there is less investment exploitation today. But there is less investment as well, and this fact simply aggravates the problem. I agree that we need guidelines, but there must be some form of arbitration. The OECD code of conduct is not very relevant, unfortunately. This is why the Community proposes an agreement on investments.

I disagree also with Dr. Frank on whether diversity among less developed countries serves as an obstacle to agreements. There is no doubt that diversity exists. But as soon as one splits up countries by continents or regions, though differences remain, the chances for agreement increase. Consider the case of Africa, for example, where the Lomé partners include an OPEC country like Nigeria, least developed countries that are extremely poor, countries like Botswana which need special provisions because of prior regional commitments, countries highly dependent on raw materials, and countries like Upper Volta which have little chance of exporting manufactured products for the next fifty years. So, opening markets to some of these countries would mean absolutely nothing.

Frank: I don't like to prolong this dialogue, but I do think I should say a few words in rebuttal.

Whenever I hear people say the problem is not that the developing countries haven't developed, but rather, the problem is the growing gap, I feel the need to have somebody demonstrate to me with simple arithmetic under what terms the absolute gap cannot grow in the short run. If the developing countries grew per year for the next few years by 20 percent a year—an unprecedented rate, historically—and we grew by 3 percent a year, the absolute gap between the rich and the poor would *enlarge*. There is no possibility of that gap contracting in the short run.

As for the fact that some of the exports of manufacturers from the developing countries are stimulated by department stores, such as Bloomingdale's in New York: I believe that we need more, not fewer such arrangements. What happens is that Bloomingdale's sends a buyer out with a sample of a shirt or something else and says to an Indian manufacturer, "Can you produce this? If you can, we'll give you an order." Now, what's wrong with that as a means of stimulating exports of manufacturers from the less developed countries? We give the design; we provide an assured market; and we help sometimes with financing and quality controls. That, it seems to me, is precisely the kind of assistance which is wanted.

As for some of the trade between the North and South being intrafirm trade: the fact of intrafirm trade doesn't take it out of the sum total of exports. The bulk of the earnings from that trade stays in the exporting country. It is paid out in wages, for local materials, and on local taxes. Of course, some profits are transferred out of the residual. So it's hard for me to see why one should separate out the intrafirm trade from the interfirm trade. I don't see the economic logic of it.

And finally, as for diversity among the developing countries: I commented on it merely to indicate in broad terms that one should be very wary of generalizing about the problems of developing countries or the policies that are appropriate to them. I wasn't saying that developing countries, because of their diversity, have any great difficulty in agreeing among themselves as to what the northern countries should do. They rarely have that kind of difficulty. As long as developing countries focus exclusively on what the North should do for the South, without any reference to what policies are in the mutual interest, including policies that may involve some difficult political decisions at home on the part of the countries of the South, there is easy agreement. But this kind of agreement is not negotiable. Mr. Pirzio-Biroli sat for a year in Paris at the Conference on International Economic Cooperation and came out with practically nothing because the Group of 77 put only this kind of agreement on the table.

Ahluwalia: I agree with a lot of what Isaiah Frank is saying, especially with his point about the importance of trade. But I disagree with the low priority he seems to assign to the whole question of resource transfers.

It is entirely true that the mechanisms of resource transfer that developing countries have pushed, for example, commodity stabilization schemes, are inefficient ways of making transfers. Yet the real problem is that the position of developed countries, reflected I fear in Dr. Frank's own statement, downplays the importance of resource transfers. While I agree that the trade issue is in the long run the most important, it is a mistake to downplay resource transfers, precisely because developing countries are so diverse.

Even if trade opportunities are opened up, it is very unlikely during at least the next ten years that many of the least developed countries will be able to benefit much from increased trading opportunities. Recent gains in manufactured exports by developing countries have been concentrated in a few countries—nations that have had the good fortune and good sense to gear their policies up to maximum exploitation of an expanding market. Malawi, unlike Brazil, is not going to find it easy to benefit from the opening up of markets in the West.

There is one other factor to consider. Within developed countries, there is a growing feeling that they will not grow as rapidly in the next twenty years as they did in the last twenty. When viewed in that context, the desire to downplay the importance of resource transfers is seen by developing countries as driving a wedge within the Third World, a wedge that may institutionalize very different levels of development and very different benefits from the existing economic order.

On the other hand, I think it is entirely right to say, after having underscored and affirmed the importance of resource transfers, "let's be sensible about how to achieve them." I think the developed countries would be quite pleased with the response they would get to a proposal making it very clear that they do not wish to phase out resource transfers, but rather to increase them and to achieve the increased level efficiently.

Frank: I accept that corrective and agree with everything Mr. Ahluwalia just said. I did not mean to downplay the importance of resource transfers but merely to place them in a broader perspective of North-South policies.

Notes

1. Jagdish Bhagwati, *The New International Economic Order: The North-South Debate* (Cambridge: M.I.T. Press, 1977).
2. David Morawetz, *Twenty-five Years of Economic Development, 1950 to 1975* (Baltimore: Johns Hopkins University Press, for the World Bank, 1977).

Bibliography

Alker, Hayward R., Bloomfield, Lincoln P., and Choucri, Nizli. *Analyzing Global Interdependence*. Cambridge, Mass.: Center for International Studies, M.I.T. 1975.

Atlantic Council Working Group on the International Monetary System. *The International Monetary System: Progress and Prospects*. Boulder, Colo.: Westview Press, 1977.

Atlantic Council Working Group on the United States and the Developing Countries. *The United States and the Developing Countries*. Boulder, Colo.: Westview Press, 1977.

Balassa, Bela. *European Economic Integration*. New York: American Elsevier Publishing Co., 1975.

Behrman, Jere R. *International Commodity Agreements: An Evaluation of the UNCTAD Integrated Commodity Programme*. Washington, D.C.: Overseas Development Council, 1977.

Bergsten, C. Fred. *The Future of the International Economic Order: An Agenda for Research*. Lexington, Mass.: Lexington Books, D.C. Heath, 1973.

Bergsten, C. Fred, Horst, Thomas, and Moran, Theodore H. *American Multinationals and American Interests*. Washington, D.C.: The Brookings Institution, 1978.

Bergsten, C. Fred, and Krause, Lawrence B., eds. *World Politics and International Economics*. Washington, D.C.: The Brookings Institution, 1975.

Bernstein, Edward M., et al. *Reflections on Jamaica*. Princeton: International Finance Section, Princeton University, 1976.

Bhagwati, J., ed. *The New International Economic Order: The North-South Debate*. Cambridge, Mass.: M.I.T. Press, 1977.

Blackhurst, Richard, Marian, Nicolas, and Tumlir, Jan. *Trade Liberalization, Protectionism and Interdependence*. Geneva: GATT, 1977.

———. *Adjustment, Trade and Growth in Developed and Developing Countries*. Geneva: GATT, 1978.

Cairncross, Alec, ed., *Economic Policy for the European Community: The Way Forward*. London: Macmillan, 1974.

Chace, James, and Ravenal, Earl C., eds. *Atlantis Lost: U.S.-European Relations After the Cold War*. New York: New York University Press for the Council on Foreign Relations, 1976.

Cline, William R. *International Monetary Reform and the Developing Countries*. Washington, D.C.: The Brookings Institution, 1976.

Cohen, Benjamin J. *Organizing the World's Money*. New York: Basic Books, 1977.

Coombes, David. *Politics and Bureaucracy in the European Community.* London: Allen and Unwin, 1970.

Cooper, Richard N. *Economic Mobility and National Economic Policy* (Wicksell Lecture, 1973). Stockholm: Almqvist and Wicksell International, 1974.

————. "Economic Interdependence and Foreign Policy in the Seventies." *World Politics* 24 (1972): 159-81.

————. *The Economics of Interdependence.* New York: McGraw-Hill Book Co., 1968.

————. "A New International Economic Order for Mutual Gain."*Foreign Policy* 26 (1977): 66-120.

————. "Trade and Monetary Relations between the United States and Western Europe." In *Western Europe: The Trials of Partnership*, edited by David S. Landes. Lexington, Mass.: Lexington Books, D.C. Heath, 1976.

Corden, W.M. "Expansion of the World Economy and the Duties of Surplus Countries." *The World Economy* 1 (1978): 121-34.

Crozier, Michel. "Structural Evolution in Industrialized Societies," and "Comment" by Anne O. Krueger. In *From Marshall Plan to Global Interdependence,* by the Organization for Economic Cooperation and Development. Paris: OECD, 1978.

Dolman, Anthony J., and van Ettinger, Jan, eds. *Partners in Tomorrow: Strategies for a New International Order.* New York: E.P. Dutton, 1978.

Erb, Guy F., and Kallab, Valeriana, eds. *Beyond Dependency: The Developing World Speaks Out.* Washington, D.C.: Overseas Development Council, 1975.

Fishlow, Albert, et al. *Rich and Poor Nations in the World Economy.* New York: McGraw-Hill for the Council on Foreign Relations, 1978.

Galtung, Johan. *The European Community: A Superpower in the Making.* Copenhagen: Christian Ejlers Forlag, 1972.

Geiger, Theodore. *Transatlantic Relations in the Prospect of an Enlarged European Community.* London: British-North American Committee, 1970.

Haas, E.B. *The Uniting of Europe: Political, Social, and Economic Forces, 1950-1957.* Stanford: Stanford University Press, 1968.

Helleiner, G.K. ed. *A World Divided: The Less Developed Countries in the International Economy.* Cambridge, England: Cambridge University Press, 1976.

Helleiner, G.K. *World Market Imperfections and the Developing Countries.* Washington, D.C.: Overseas Development Council, 1978.

Hoffman, Stanley, "Domestic Politics and Interdependence." In *From Marshall Plan to Global Interdependence,* by the Organization for Economic Cooperation and Development. Paris: OECD, 1978.

Hoffman, Stanley. "Uneven Allies: An Overview." In *Western Europe: The Trials of Partnership,* edited by David Landes. Lexington, Mass.: Lexington Books, D.C. Heath, 1976.

Keohane, Robert O., and Nye, Joseph S., Jr. *Transnational Relations and World Politics.* Cambridge, Mass.: Harvard University Press, 1972.

_____. *Power and Interdependence.* Boston: Little Brown & Co., 1977.

Kindleberger, Charles P. "The OECD and the Third World." In *From Marshall Plan to Global Interdependence,* by the Organization for Economic Cooperation and Development. Paris: OECD, 1978.

Krause, Lawrence B., and Salant, Walter S., eds. *World Wide Inflation: Theory and Recent Experience.* Washington, D.C.: The Brookings Institution, 1977.

Landes, David S., ed. *Western Europe: The Trials of Partnership.* Lexington, Mass.: Lexington Books, D.C. Heath, 1976.

Laszlo, Ervin, et al. *The Objectives of the New International Economic Order.* New York: Pergamon Press for United Nations Institute for Training and Research, 1978.

Leontief, Wassily; Carter, Anne P.; and Petri, Peter A. *The Future of the World Economy.* New York: Oxford University Press for the United Nations, 1977.

Lerner, D., and Gorden, M. *Euro-Atlantica: Changing Perspectives of European Elites.* Boston: MIT Press, 1969.

Lewis, W. Arthur. *The Evolution of the International Economic Order.* Princeton: Princeton University Press, 1978.

Lindbeck, Assar. "Economic Dependence and Interdependence in the Industrialized World," and "Comment" by W. Max Corden. In *From Marshall Plan to Global Interdependence,* by the Organization for Economic Cooperation and Development. Paris: OECD, 1978.

_____. "Stabilization Policy in Open Economies With Endogenous Politicians," *American Economic Review Papers and Proceedings* 66 (1976): 1-19.

Lindberg, L.N., and Scheingold, S.A. *Europe's Would-Be Polity, Patterns of Change in the European Community.* Englewood Cliffs, N.J.: Prentice-Hall, 1970.

Machlup, Fritz, ed. *Economic Integration: Worldwide, Regional, Sectoral.* London: Macmillan Co. for the International Economic Association, 1976.

Maillet, Pierre. *The Construction of a European Community: Achievements and Prospects for the Future.* New York: Praeger, 1977.

Mally, Gerhard. *The European Community in Perspective.* Lexington, Mass.: Lexington Books, D.C. Heath, for Atlantic Council of the United States, 1973.

_____. *Interdependence.* Lexington, Mass.: Lexington Books, D.C. Heath, for Atlantic Council of the United States, 1976.

————, ed. *The New Europe and the United States.* Lexington, Mass.: Lexington Books, D.C. Heath, for Atlantic Council of the United States, 1974.

Organization for Economic Cooperation and Development. *From Marshall Plan to Global Interdependence.* Paris: OECD, 1978.

————. *Towards Full Employment and Price Stability.* Paris: OECD, 1977.

Sasse, Christoph, et al. *Decision Making in the European Community.* New York: Praeger, 1977.

Schaetzel, J. Robert. *The Unhinged Alliance: America and the European Community.* New York: Harper & Row for the Council on Foreign Relations, 1975.

Singh, Jyoti Shankar. *A New International Economic Order.* New York: Praeger, 1977.

Shonfield, Andrew, ed. *International Economic Relations of the Western World, 1959-1971.* London: Oxford University Press for the Royal Institute of International Affairs, 1976.

Sjöstedt, Gunnar. *The External Role of the European Community.* Lexington, Mass.: Lexington Books, D.C. Heath, 1977.

Solomon, Robert. *The Interdependence of Nations: An Agenda for Research.* Washington, D.C.: National Science Foundation, 1977.

————. *The International Monetary System, 1945-76: An Insider's View.* New York: Harper & Row, 1977.

Tinbergen, Jan, coord. *Reshaping the International Order: A Report to the Club of Rome.* New York: E.P. Dutton, 1976.

Tollison, Robert D., and Willett, Thomas D. *Problems of Economic Interdependence: A Public Choice Perspective.* Unpublished manuscript.

Trezise, Philip H. *The Atlantic Connection.* Washington, D.C.: The Brookings Institution, 1975.

Vernon, Raymond. "Critical Choices: The Structure of Industry," In *Western Europe: The Trials of Partnership,* edited by David S. Landes. Lexington, Mass.: Lexington Books, D.C. Heath, 1976.

————. *Storm over the Multinationals: The Real Issues.* Cambridge, Mass.: Harvard University Press, 1977.

Whitman, Marina v.N. "Coordination and Management of the International Economy: A Search for Organizing Principles." In *Contemporary Economic Problems,* edited by William Fellner. Washington, D.C.: American Enterprise Institute for Public Policy Research, 1977.

————. "International Interdependence and the U.S. Economy," In *Contemporary Economic Problems,* edited by William Fellner. Washington, D.C.: American Enterprise Institute for Public Policy Research, 1976.

————. "Leadership Without Hegemony: Our Role in the World Economy." *Foreign Policy* 20 (1975): 138-60.

_____. "The Locomotive Approach to Sustaining World Recovery: Has It Run Out of Steam?" In *Contemporary Economic Problems,* edited by William Fellner. Washington, D.C.: American Enterprise Institute for Public Policy Research, 1978.

_____. *Sustaining the International Economic System: Issues for U.S. Policy.* Princeton: International Finance Section, Princeton University, 1977.

Index

About the Contributors

Montek S. Ahluwalia is senior economist with the Development Research Center of the World Bank.

Martin Bangemann is a Free Democrat member of the West German Parliament and until recently a member of the European Parliament; he is also a member of the Executive Committee of the European Federation of Liberals and Democrats.

Ranieri Bombassei is a cabinet member to the deputy director general for external relations in the Commission of the European Communities.

Alan Cranston is the senior senator from California and majority whip in the United States Senate.

Francesco Forte is professor of fiscal economics and director, University of Turin, Italy.

Isaiah Frank is William L. Clayton professor of international economics at The Johns Hopkins University School of Advanced International Studies.

Makato Hara at the time of the conference was chief economist, Bank of Tokyo Limited, New York.

Steven Koblik is associate professor of history and chairman, International Relations Program, Pomona College.

David Marquand, former Labor member of the British Parliament, until recently was chief advisor, Secretariat-General of the Commission of the European Community.

Gerald M. Meier is professor of International Economics, Stanford University.

Schelto Patijn is Labor member of the Second Chamber of the States General of the Netherlands and until recently a member of the European Parliament.

Corrado Pirzio-Biroli is financial advisor at the European Communities' delegation to the United States.

J. Robert Schaetzel, a writer and consultant, was U.S. Ambassador to the European Communities from 1966 to 1972.

Sir Christopher Soames, former British cabinet minister and British ambassador to France, was vice-president of the Commission of the European Communities responsible for external relations, 1973-77.

Robert Solomon is a senior fellow in the Foreign Policy Studies Program at the Brookings Institution.

Fernand Spaak is head of the delegation of the Commission of the European Communities to the United States government.

About the Editor

Gordon K. Douglass, a teacher and writer in the fields of international economics and higher education, is the James Irvine professor of economics at Pomona College and the Claremont Graduate School. He also is chairman of the department of economics at Pomona College.

The codirector (with Steven Koblik) of the conference on the new interdependence which generated the idea for this book, Dr. Douglass's explorations of the boundaries between international economics, international politics, and diplomatic history, reach back in time to the period when he coordinated development of the concentration in international relations at Pomona College, one of America's most successful liberal arts college programs.

A magna cum laude graduate of Pomona College, he earned the Ph.D. degree in industrial economics from the Massachusetts Institute of Technology in 1963. Since then, while teaching at the California Institute of Technology and in Claremont, he has written several books, articles, and notes on themes related to the new interdependence, including recently *Investment in Learning* (Jossy-Bass, 1978) in collaboration with Howard Bowen. The Ford Foundation, the Lilly Endowment, the Haynes Foundation and the Irvine Foundation have helped to support his research and study in these areas. Dr. Douglass also is director of a program in "Food, Land, and Power: Agriculture in a Changing World Order", being supported at Pomona College by The Kellogg Foundation.